VW ADVERTISING

The art of selling the air-cooled Volkswagens

VW ADVERTISING

The art of selling the air-cooled Volkswagens

BY RICHARD COPPING

Herridge & Sons

Published in 2014 by
Herridge & Sons Ltd
Lower Forda, Shebbear
Devon EX21 5SY

ISBN 978-1-906133-63-4
Printed in China

CONTENTS

INTRODUCTION

Although the car we know as the Beetle was born of Hitler's desire to provide cheap transport for the masses and Ferdinand Porsche's lifelong ambition to design such a vehicle, the only tangible post-war asset of the Nazi era was the factory built to produce it. An urgent need for vehicles to support the military government and the ingenuity of the factory's temporary guardian, Englishman Ivan Hirst, ensured it was neither stripped of its contents nor demolished.

In January 1948, ex-Opel director Heinz Nordhoff arrived at what was now known as Wolfsburg in preparation for returning the Volkswagenwerk to German ownership. Nordhoff was destined to stay with Volkswagen until his death in April 1968, and it was through his skill, determination,

attention to detail and sheer hard work that the manufacturer grew to be one of the largest in the world, surpassed only by Detroit-based Ford and General Motors. By 1965, Nordhoff presided over a company whose workforce produced in excess of 1,000,000 cars of the same type each year. Meanwhile, a basic message behind the company's advertising asked, "Why is the Volkswagen a favourite in 136 countries?"

Throughout the 1950s demand for the Beetle exceeded production, no matter what steps were taken to increase yearly output. Wisely, Nordhoff had avoided being sidetracked into production of costly-to-produce and niche-market variations on the Beetle theme. Thus, the soft-top four-seater version was handed to coachbuilder

Updated version of early "Das Cabriolet" brochure issued in 1951 and 1952.

Wilhelm Karmann of Osnabruck, as was a sporty-bodied Beetle designed by Ghia of Turin – appropriately dubbed the Karmann Ghia. Nordhoff's only exception was the commercially more viable Transporter, launched in November 1949. Completely new in concept, the multi-variant Transporter was so successful that by 1956 it warranted its own factory in Hanover, and within 12 years had also achieved the magic million.

While demand for Volkswagen's products remained strong, Nordhoff took the view that replacement would be a mistake. During a 1958 speech, which equally could have been delivered nearly a decade later, Nordhoff summed up his philosophy and the challenge presented to those promoting the same products for the best part of 20 years: "I have decided to stick to the policy that has served us so well. Based on Professor Porsche's original design, the Volkswagen of today looks almost exactly like the prototype model that was produced more than 20 years ago, but every single part of this car has been refined and improved over the years – these will continue to be our 'model changes'."

Nordhoff had supervised the launch of what was known as the Export Model Beetle in the summer of 1949. Mechanically identical to its forebears, the De Luxe carried a trim level and quality of finish unrecognisable to the shoddy work of earlier years, making the Beetle a genuinely saleable commodity across the world. The Transporter, new to the market a few months later, was produced in a manner guaranteed to satisfy from the start.

Although essentially an engineer and out of step with the frivolity of advertising, Nordhoff demanded his products should be sold in the best possible way. From the stimulating but uncoordinated publications of 1949, inspirational artwork from the brush of Bernd Reuters soon resulted in a catalogue of material unequalled by any other manufacturer. Supplemented by near perfect photography and, as the years went by, the increased presence of other artists, the style established at the beginning of the decade remained constant to its end.

As the 1960s dawned, Nordhoff felt confident that he could add a further model without jeopardising Beetle or Transporter production. This was the now largely-overlooked VW 1500, a bigger two-door saloon or estate.

Interestingly, it was the US market that was to transform Volkswagen's advertising only a short time before the 1500's launch. Faced with increasingly serious inroads into their market from the German manufacturer, Ford and General Motors declared intentions to produce smaller cars to compete with the Volkswagen. Carl Hahn, a protégé of Nordhoff's, and recently appointed to head Volkswagen of America, determined that for the first time he must advertise the company's products to retain market share. His choice of agency for the Beetle, after sitting through countless dull presentations, was radical. Doyle Dane Bernbach (DDB) was

a relative newcomer, with a style that flew in the face of convention. Stark but stunningly clever photography, and succinct yet incredibly witty and thought-provoking text, transformed the look of Volkswagen's brochures. Such was the impact of the DDB's work that not only did it help to lift the Beetle to near-cult status, it forced other manufacturers to follow suit.

In summer 1967 the Beetle underwent sufficient changes for it to be marketed as "the new Beetle", while the 17-

From in-house magazine "VW Information" – Heinz Nordhoff in typical publicity pose at the centre of another expansion programme.

Its running costs? Low.

Eye-catching photography became a standard feature as the 1960s unfolded.

year run of the first-generation Transporter came to an end. Its replacement – a vehicle considerably altered in appearance but carrying many of the characteristics of its predecessor – confounded Nordhoff's critics, who complained that he was incapable of changing model. Ongoing improvements to the VW 1500 (which became the VW 1600 over the years 1965/6) ensured the latest versions demonstrated many changes, while when Nordhoff died in April 1968, plans were advanced to launch an even larger Volkswagen, the VW 411.

Sadly, Nordhoff's passing saw the company placed in the hands of Kurt Lotz, an individual without experience in the motor industry but eager to carry out the wishes of his political masters. Following Germany's first post-war recession of autumn 1966, Nordhoff had spoken out against a government acting unfavourably towards the motor industry. Inevitably, the politicians (who owned a part of Volkswagen anyway) fought back. According to the most vociferous, Nordhoff had, "produced too many cars and too few ideas", as well as, "the wrong models". Pressure was brought on Nordhoff to retire, and Lotz joined Volkswagen as his

deputy in June 1967.

With Nordhoff out of the way, Lotz demonstrated his true colours. Within months, if not weeks, he was speaking of Volkswagen as, "immovable under a single director for the past 20 years". He told any audience willing to listen that the only way forward was destroy the past as quickly as possible, and spoke openly of Volkswagen's only chance for survival being a new car. Regrettably, his words were not backed by action.

No Beetle replacement appeared during Lotz's four-year reign. Instead, frightened by US health and safety legislation, he spent a fortune on updating the car, giving it a revised front end, MacPherson strut suspension, a bigger boot, and the unfortunate accolade of being described by cynics as the pregnant Beetle. Befuddled thinking ensured that the 1302S Beetle, or Super Beetle, answered none of the potential safety issues. One of Lotz's final acts was to sanction further development, endowing the Super Beetle with a curved windscreen and a plastic dashboard. This would have been significant if the USA hadn't by then backtracked on its safety plans!

Lotz launched one new car during his time in office. Having bought NSU, he re-badged the soon-to-be-launched K70 model as a VW. With its uncompromising three-box shape it looked anonymous and produced an appalling drag coefficient of 0.51 that guaranteed heavy fuel consumption. Coupled with a catalogue of other faults, including poor engine reliability and overheating, not to mention premature rusting, this was a Volkswagen like no other. Lotz compounded his sins by selling the K70 at a low margin to compete with the group's Audi 100 and VW 411E.

Against the background of rapidly falling profits and lack of a genuine Beetle replacement, Lotz was ousted by trouble-shooter and long-time Volkswagen group employee Rudolph Leiding in 1971. Volkswagen's third Director General set about his task with relish. Recognising that Lotz had damaged Volkswagen's greatest asset beyond repair, he quickly devised plans to replace the full range of Nordhoff's air-cooled models.

The first of the new generation of water-cooled, front-wheel-drive models was the 1973 Passat, a derivative of Audi's highly successful 80. The replacement for the Karmann Ghia, the Scirocco, followed in the early months of 1974, as Leiding's sporty-bodied way to test the water for the forthcoming Golf. July 1974 marked the Golf's official debut, although Beetle production, exiled from Wolfsburg, continued in Germany at the Emden factory.

A general economic downturn required Leiding to introduce a cheaper model than the Golf as a second Beetle successor. Again he turned to Audi, re-badging its 50 as the Polo in the early spring of 1975. Leiding's plans to replace Nordhoff's second-generation Transporter took lowest priority. Despite its thirst for fuel, exacerbated by fitting successively larger engines, the Transporter remained a stalwart for Volkswagen.

Although Leiding was Volkswagen's saviour in the 1970s, the losses he created through his enormous investment programme were not excused by an increasingly concerned supervisory board. After initially increasing profits from the low point of the Lotz era to DM86 million in 1972 and DM109 million the following year, in 1974 Volkswagen experienced its first loss, when it was a substantial DM555 million in the red. After Leiding's early 1975 departure the loss shrank to DM145 million, while his successor, ex-Ford man Toni Schmücker, basked in the glory of a DM784 million profit in 1976.

July 1973 saw the end of production of the VW 1600, followed a year later by the last of the VW 412 models. Production of a greatly truncated Beetle range ended on 19 January 1978, although Mexican imports were ready and waiting to take their place. Karmann's Beetle Cabriolet lingered until a soft-top version of the Golf was ready to replace it in January 1980. Nordhoff's second-generation Transporter bowed out in the summer of 1979, and finally in August 1985 the last batch of Mexican-built Beetles arrived on German soil.

Curiously, Volkswagen's strategy with brochures and advertising appeared to change with the dawn of the 1970s, just as it had a decade before. Gone was the adventurous and instantly eye-catching photography, banished was the scene-setting cover, and exiled was the wittiest copy. In their collective places was a more austere style, reflecting the air of a giant in crisis and dividing opinion. The move to single-colour covers, with or without the relief of a car, could well stimulate a designer's love of subtle simplicity. Big pictures, stripped of activity and minimalistic text, relieved of wit in favour of clarity, might well appeal to those favouring the fashionable clinical look of today.

Fortunately for those who were not enamoured by the latest approach, Volkswagen of America opted to stay firmly rooted in the style of the 1960s, just as the brand's followers would reject the VW Rabbit (Golf) as a worthy successor to the venerable Beetle.

August 1971 – witness to a much starker design for European brochures.

BEGINNINGS: THE KDF-WAGEN

With the wealth of the state at their disposal and the art of propaganda perfected, the Nazis' literature to promote Hitler's "car for everyman" project was lavishly presented and rich in political endorsement.

The first to be published, in 1938, revealed the Nazis' control over vehicle supplies, with a harsh savings scheme imposed on would-be purchasers. Instead of altruistically motorising the German people, the brochure described the machine not as a volks-wagen but as a Kraft-durch-Freude wagen (translated as "strength-through-joy car"), reflecting the Nazi-created KdF, a state body that organised recreation, travel, sport and leisure within the Reich.

While enticing images were designed to imply a bond between the KdF-Wagen owner and their car, the key message was of the vehicle being Hitler's own creation, manufactured in a purpose-built factory that he designed personally. Inside the 32-page brochure, the text (including words of the Führer) emphasised that here was carefully-crafted propaganda, however generous the descriptions of the KdF-Wagen's attributes.

"The KdF-Wagen – produced at the command of the Führer.

"While the automobile remains the preserve of the upper classes, it will be difficult to remove its class-denoting character as well as its divisive class-splitting nature. That is why

The 1938/39 brochure, with front cover showing the savings book required to attain a KdF-Wagen. The heading, "Your KdF-Wagen" implied state benevolence, while the mountainous background of the back cover suggested reliability and a freedom to roam that was previously impossible for all but the wealthy.

the car will be made available for all."

Bearing in mind that the KdF-Wagen hadn't entered series production when war broke out, publication of Der KdF-Wagen von A bis Z – to all extents and purposes a handbook for owners – appears odd. However, extending to 124 highly detailed pages, its value as a marketing tool was immense. Carefully composed to discuss all aspects of ownership, even washing and polishing the KdF-Wagen, it served as a rallying call to join the Nazis' savings scheme or as a deterrent to anyone contemplating an already-available vehicle.

Among 1939's deluge of additional material, the most interesting was designed to coincide with the arrival of the annual Berlin automobile show. The cover ingeniously lacked anything more than a small, embossed KdF-Wagen, backed by a swastika surrounded by rays of sunlight. Inside, the majority was devoted to a series of costly acetates that, with fascinating see-through clarity, slowly stripped the complete KdF-Wagen to nothing more than a chassis, engine, gearbox and petrol tank. An index-style technical specification followed. Without undertones of Führer worship and lacking text, which many non German-speaking visitors to the show would have failed to understand, this brochure was possibly the Reich's first attempt to raise awareness of the KdF-Wagen as export material.

Propaganda value for the Führer and his regime.

The car worth saving for.

A cathedral to Nazism – the KdF factory.

A KdF saver's bible of desire, the 124-page "Der KdF-Wagen von A bis Z".

Centre spread of "Der KdF-Wagen von A bis Z" confirms the multitude of subject headings the Nazis contrived to write about

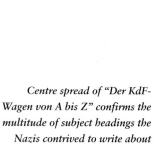

The Nazis also issued a traditional eight-page brochure in 1938, relying on artwork rather than photography and employing tactics of exaggeration favoured by post-war Volkswagen artists.

Der Kdf Wagen

No expense spared. Glossy acetate layers formed ever-diminishing cutaway images of the KdF-Wagen.

THE 1950S

Engaging Gear

With the arrival of the De Luxe (or Export) Beetle and introduction of the Karmann Cabriolet and Hebmüller Coupé in summer 1949, followed by the launch of the Transporter in November the same year, Volkswagen needed to ensure that appropriate sales literature was available to promote each model. Money was far from plentiful, for Nordhoff ploughed as much as he could into refinement of the Beetle and development of the Transporter. However, to skimp on sales material would have been unrealistic.

Although lacking a coordinated approach, two styles of presentation were evident in the 1949 output. First, in keeping with material produced by other manufacturers, were brochures that relied on artwork rather than photography to provide impact.

The other approach was photography-led throughout. Colour predominated, but as examples of literature dating from 1950 show, such practice was by no means universal. Text was short and to the point.

"Der Volkswagen", also available with English text, portrayed the export Beetle on its front and rear covers. In neither instance was the car's lines drawn in a fashion designed to flatter. The profile of the wheels and tyres might suggest a chunkier profile, but items specific to the export market upgrade, such as the bumpers and wing trim details, were underplayed.

Conversely, beautifully message-ridden thumbnail artwork peppered one of the internal pages, depicting the Beetle on the Autobahn, climbing its way through rugged countryside and heading the pack at traffic lights. Elsewhere were two full-page, carefully cropped black-and-white images, one of the export model, the other of the standard. The De Luxe was placed on a pale green background, and the designer added white outlines of a crowd of well-heeled admirers. Significantly, the basic Beetle was accompanied by an outline of the Wolfsburg factory.

Rather than lengthy, turgid copy, the prose was short and reasonably pithy, as illustrated by headings that comprised the only words on two separate pages.

1949 "Volkswagen Cabriolet 4 Sitzer" was photography-led, the only deviations being sympathetic sketches of details like the vehicle's dashboard and rear seat storage area. Hints of studio enhancement were apparent, and nowhere more so than in the cover image, which was doctored to include a smaller-than-life female driver. The short text fell under four headings, loosely interpreted thus: An imposing elegance; Coachbuilt desirability; A surprising amount of room; A genuine Volkswagen.

Produced entirely in black and white, this brochure depicted the impressive Wolfsburg factory on its cover, and included images of the giant presses and production line. Rows of Beetles were shown ready for despatch, plus a Nordhoff special, a photograph depicting a VW dealership's service department. The vehicles outlined and pictured included the Transporter in Delivery Van and Micro Bus guise, as well as the new introduction to the Beetle range (circa April 1950), the fold-back sunroof model.

1950 "VW-Lieferwagen, Eine Bildserie" offered exactly what the cover indicated: a series of photographs intended to promote the merits of the Delivery Van, Kombi and Micro Bus. Of most interest has to be extensive use of material depicting prototypes rather than production models. Curiously, the first caption related to two-colour paint, a feature not available from the factory. However, Transporters could be ordered in primer for owners to organise painting in company liveries, a theme that would become significant in Transporter marketing.

In some instances, brochures first produced in 1949 were either carried forward or subtly updated (a practice that would inevitably persist over the years). One such was the Hebmüller coupé brochure, or in the parlance of the day, Volkswagen's 2 Sitzer Cabriolet. The version reproduced here dates from February 1950; production faded away in March, so it is likely that many a brochure simply went to waste. The 2 Sitzer Cabriolet brochure was near identical to the one promoting the four-seater model. Text was minimal, with colour photography designed to enrapture.

An unnamed artist presented a most attractive cover for a small (149x105mm) multi-page brochure in 1950, which outlined many aspects of every Volkswagen's make-up. Although this publication appeared dedicated to the Beetle, it related to the Transporter as well, perhaps illustrating that the marketing of the larger vehicle hadn't yet been fully developed. Of greatest significance was the page listing the models covered by the brochure, while an address book-style indicator gave access to the following topics: motor, make-up of the engine, air and oil cooling, clutch, transmission, gearbox, rear axle, chassis frame, front axle, steering, body, warm-air heating, engine accessories, maintenance and care.

The Volkswagen models listed were VW Sedan (standard model); VW Sedan (export model); sunroof models of each (manufactured by Golde); VW Van (with box body); VW Kombi (for passenger and cargo transportation); VW Micro Bus (for eight people).

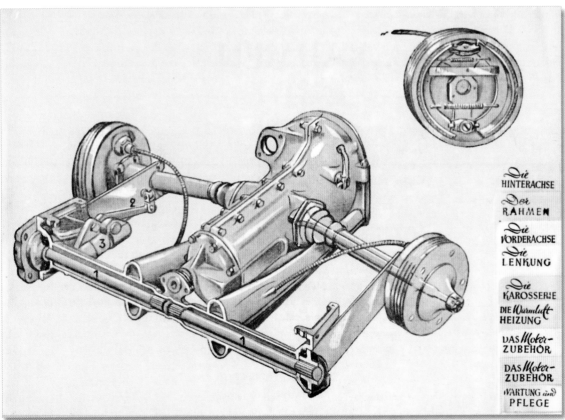

Proof is lacking, but it appears likely that the dual-language examples of a brochure dating from 1950 originated through the Belgian importer, D'Leteren Brothers. Small print on the back of the six-page foldout brochure assigned the work to OTP, the Office Technique de Publicité, 40 Rue de L'Ecuyer, Bruxelles.

The unnamed artist clearly struggled with perspective when it came to the Transporter's front. Nor could he successfully convey window glass, while the scale of the individual loading the vehicle was totally out of proportion to its size.

Inside, it would appear that a different artist was asked to create images of the Transporter in use, and borrowed images of prototype vehicles to create his masterpieces. Finally, in line with Wolfsburg's pride in its premises, a full page was devoted to a stylised drawing of the factory.

The text proved particularly interesting, being clear that Nordhoff's message of a multi-purpose vehicle had been fully understood. Amazingly, considering the year (emblazoned on the front of each vehicle), the notion of the Transporter being converted for use as a weekend or holiday camper was well ahead of its time.

It said, "A Thousand Possible Uses. The great strength of the Volkswagen Van and the generous design of its interior opens possibilities of many different uses. In addition to its use as a Delivery Van (transport of food, milk, bread, vegetables, etc.), the Volkswagen Transporter can be used as a small bus, mobile workshop, travelling shop, or as any of the following: ambulance, camping car, radio or speaker van, postal vehicle, etc."

Welcome Herr Reuters

With the arrival of the De Luxe (or export) Beetle and introduction of the Karmann Cabriolet and Hebmüller Coupé in summer 1949, followed by the launch of the Transporter in November the same year, Volkswagen needed to ensure that appropriate sales literature was available to promote each model. Money was far from plentiful, for Nordhoff ploughed as much as he could into refinement of the Beetle and development of the Transporter. However, to skimp on sales material would have been unrealistic.

Although the hotchpotch of brochure styles might be deemed sufficient for a company in its infancy, a coordinated approach, employing the skills of a top professional, was preferred if Volkswagen's standard of promotion was to match its rival manufacturers in Europe and beyond. During 1950, Beetle sales escalated to 81,979 cars from a little over 46,000 the year before. The Transporter attracted 8059 purchasers and would soon command many

more. Nordhoff's Volkswagen was on the move.

There is a lack of clarity regarding the exact date of Bernd Reuters's first association with Volkswagen and his role or commission. What can be stated unequivocally is that the work of this already-renowned artist would shape Volkswagen's advertising for the best part of a decade, despite Reuters's death in 1958.

Bernhard Wilhelm Joseph Reuters was born on 11 September 1901. Following brief training at Berlin's art school, the lure of a regular income was sufficient for Reuters to become an illustrator for the Scherl-Verlag group, whose titles included the journal Sport im Bild. Among his tasks was illustration of the serialised work of Erich Maria Remarque, later to become one of Germany's most famous authors.

Bernd Reuters's style, though inevitably refined and perfected in later years, was instantly recognisable as sympathetic to the in-vogue Art Deco movement. Apart from perfecting representations of light and shade and, in automotive terms, gleaming paintwork and highly polished chromework, Reuters made use of rich colour and bold lines. As a way of adding appeal, he invariably depicted modern young ladies behind the wheel or beside a car.

Additionally, he would portray cars driving through all sorts of conditions, during daylight hours and at night, come storm or sun. His cars would climb the steepest of roads one moment and form a reflection on a wet pavement the next. Essentially, he brought his subject to life on the page, and proved invaluable to all who engaged his remarkable talent. Above all, others emulated his style but never bettered it.

Initially, Reuters signed his work in capital script, although by August 1925 he had changed to the flowing style well known in later work. The following year he added an abbreviated date, something he may have picked up while in London. An early example of this style survives, the subject being a street scene of the British capital, including a London bus.

Between 1924 and 1931, Reuters's work appeared on the cover of Sport im Bild seven times, an achievement bettered by nine illustrations for the magazine MoTor between 1927 and 1932, including 1928 and 1931 international motor show editions. From 1926, Reuters also produced what might be described as his first specific brand advertising material. This was for the GDA (Gemeinschaft Deutscher Automobilfabriken or Association of German Carmakers), a reasonably loose association of Berlin-based NAG, Hansa and the Brandenburg company, Brennabor. At the time, Brennabor was second only to Opel in terms of production volume.

From there, work opened up with the tyre manufacturer Continental (where Reuters designed covers for the in-house magazine), film and photo giant Agfa, sparkling wine specialist Henkell, and Siemens, the household appliance firm.

Reuters's first love soon became evident as he accepted more commissions from car manufacturers. In 1928 he carried out work for Elite (whose Diamond works were acquired by Opel in the same year), the following year for the US firm Graham-Paige, and in 1930 for the Lincoln Motor Company. Reuters added Eagle and Horch to his portfolio in 1931, while coveted work for Opel and Rohr followed in 1932. The following year, commissions for Horch extended to other brands within Auto Union, namely Audi, DKW and Wanderer, an exercise repeated in 1938. In 1937, Reuters worked for Adler, producing a series of adverts and a brochure for its 2.5-litre Eagle, a car with streamlined bodywork particularly suited to Reuters's recognisable style.

In an interview given to a Swiss magazine in 1951, Reuters alluded to work for the British market, the first of which appears to date from 1935. Although he professed to not remember all the makes, he mentioned, "Amstrong Sidenlie, Rols Royce and Woelsie" (sic), suggesting the projects had been completed without the need to travel to Britain. By way of confirmation, the cover of The Autocar dated 24 April 1936 featured Reuters's illustration of the new Wolseley 10 and 12. The most quirky, however, was the advert for Morris of either 1936 or '37 vintage, which included Reuters's signature as a mirror image. Clearly the artwork had to be inverted to overcome the problem of a steering wheel on the opposite side.

The rapid growth in the artist's portfolio was consistent with Reuters's increasingly apparent interest in automotive design. Articles such as *New Car Outlines* and *Perfection of Appearance*, published in 1928 and 1929 respectively, might be described as preambles for a fully illustrated piece published in *Motor* in 1932 under the title, *Motorised Carriage – Streamlined Car*. To describe what appeared in *Sport im Bild* as a paper rather than a simple story might be apt, as on this occasion Reuters extended his thoughts from body and interior design towards a vehicle's chassis, engine and even its drive.

As Germany fell under the spell of Hitler and his Nazi party, Reuters could easily have been in danger because his

The definitive pose of the early 1950s (From untitled brochure dated June 1953).

maternal grandfather was Jewish; fortunately, he survived. The indications are that as the war progressed he found work harder to come by, and he suffered a blow when his Berlin studio was destroyed in a 1943 air raid. Lost forever were a host of original drawings and sketches. Personally unscathed, Reuters deserted the city in favour of more rural Brandenburg and Neuglobsow. However, with the war over he moved once more, this time relocating to Hamburg.

Perhaps inevitably, the immediate post-war period proved slow for Reuters, but by 1949 a decided upturn had taken place, with a commission from Ford-Werke in Cologne proving most significant. Towards the end of 1950, or conceivably at the start of 1951, Reuters became associated with Volkswagen for the first time. Before the war, no manufacturer had been successful in securing exclusive use of the artist's talents, although it is possible that nobody asked. It appears that Reuters's role at Volkswagen, at least initially, was of a more all-embracing nature than it had been for other manufacturers, encompassing the design of VW's stand at motor shows and, conceivably, advice on body and interior aesthetics. Even so, there is no evidence that Reuters was on Volkswagen's payroll; indeed, the inability of the company's archive department to find much material relating to him suggests he remained a freelance, or ran his own studio throughout.

Two helpful, if not conclusive, articles about Bernd Reuters and his work appeared in Volkswagen's in-house publication, VW Information. The first was published in 1955; the second, his obituary, more or less a verbatim reprint of the original, followed in 1958. Reuters suffered a fatal heart attack during the early hours of 6 July 1958. He was only 56 and had no previous history of heart disease.

Although somewhat florid in the style of the day, the obituary helps us to understand the man who lives on through his outstanding interpretations of the Beetle, Transporter and Karmann Ghia.

"His name means something in the world of automobiles, and that says a little about someone who was neither an engineer nor a salesman, but an artist. His name means something in the world of graphic art, and this in turn says a lot about a man who neither exhibited at exhibitions, nor turned figurative, landscape, or modern-abstract cartwheels, but who concentrated his entire life on one thing: the face of the automobile and its artistic representation. Many a person who met him for the first time may have asked himself the question as to why a man of such spirit and such well-grounded knowledge had restricted himself to using his God-given gift in such a narrow area of industrial technology, instead of dedicating his talent to the depiction of a variety of things and people, events and situations and choosing his subjects randomly. But those who have become more familiar with Bernd Reuters's creativity and work know how prudent this concentration is and that it only leads to the synthesis of artist and expert.

"There are probably only half a dozen men in the whole world who simultaneously understand so much about the art of advertising and the technology and functioning of the automobile from the viewpoint of the public, as Bernd Reuters. You can therefore understand that his irreplaceable ability is really not meant as a cliché. Despite his concentration on one task, this man was so incredibly versatile that it is hard to say where his death has created the biggest gap and what we will miss most: the colleague in the advertising department who gave our catalogues and brochures their much copied and inimitable style and who, like a bloodhound, sought out quality and accuracy throughout the printing houses of Germany; or the designer who, in the area of technical development, creatively influenced lines, colours, upholstery and covers, in short all those important details to do with taste, without driving the design engineers to distraction, the man who, with equal sympathy for both sides, so often built bridges between the wishes of the sales department and the practicalities of technology; or the person in our midst whose seat is suddenly empty...

"To remain with him a little longer; in our company, whose size occasionally demands the imposition of strict demarcation of responsibilities bordering on officialdom, Bernd Reuters was actually no one's superior and no-one's underling, but many sought his advice and he was always ready to help, while many could be proud to call him their friend. He was an artist without artistic airs, but with all the characteristics of a valuable and sociable human being, never quick in his judgement, always careful to listen to and weigh up the arguments of his colleagues. Whatever he presented was always fully formed; his opinion demanded respect, not by means of suggestion or the right to artistic freedom, but through compelling presentation of all possibilities and consequences, as if he were a design engineer, not an artist.

"Never has the portrait of our friend's career been more accurately drawn than by the late Stefan von Szendsy. This is how he described Bernd Reuters in the *Aral Journal* as an interpreter of technology a few years ago:

'Bernd Reuters had something granted to so few: the gift to find his own style, from the earliest beginnings, to which he remained unerringly faithful as an expression of his own artistic touch, even though he was able to develop it to ever greater maturity.

'The industry recognised very quickly that the strong appeal emanating from Bernd Reuters's illustrations could equally draw the viewer into the spell of the advertisement. Thus, Reuters became the illustrator not only of German, but also of international automobile advertising. The most famous brands in the world competed to make use of this man's unique artistry for their own purposes ...

"Reuters's drawings, much copied, are so characteristic that they need no signature! Wherein lay Reuters's artistry? Not in the subtlety of lines in drawings, not in the strangely delicate shadows, not in the artfully arranged lights, not in the kindly composition – but in the unique synthesis of all factors of artistic design. Reuters doesn't recreate the vehicles, he doesn't treat them as portraits, but he flings the cars onto the paper as he sees them in front of his mind's eye, as he experiences their idiosyncrasies. And yet each drawing exudes the characteristics of the specific brand, of the specific car...'

"Let us now, after his death, transfer to the past what a journalist once said in the present: 'Bernd Reuters is a child of modern times; he lived in the magical sphere of technology. But, through his refined artistic means of expression he has, unlike most of us, the gift of imbuing technology with a sense of poetry which people inwardly yearn for. Such was his artistry which was his life!'"

Building the Beetle brand

Reuters's first brochure work for Volkswagen can be dated to 1950 (thanks to the absence of at least one feature introduced at the start of the following year), although a specific month after March, when the 100,000th Beetle was built (and referred to in the text) cannot be confirmed. The six-page "Das VW Cabriolet" brochure included a cover and double-spread illustration that can definitely be attributed to Reuters, plus two more unsigned images that appear to be of his style and a further couple that most likely came from the pen of another illustrator.

Virtually all the characteristics that identify the Reuters-led era were evident. In the cover image, despite a lack of sophistication associated with Reuters's later Volkswagen work, the car was elongated (note the size of the driver's door and rear quarter panel). The rounded contours of the wings (and to a lesser extent the boot lid) were exaggerated too. Subtle toning of a single colour (in this instance either black or maroon) implied a richness and depth of paint gloss usually associated with far more expensive vehicles. Air lines had been added (across the wheels and lower body) to give an impression of the Cabriolet cutting through the atmosphere in the manner of a sports car, while the size of the driver (notably female – the target market) was reduced to give the illusion of a more spacious interior.

With its comb binder, four full-size lift-out images, a separate 16-page booklet equivalent to a technical specification, a silver cover and embossed title, the de luxe format 1951 brochure helped confirm the look of the Beetle for future Reuters-led Beetle publications. Although it is unlikely that Reuters contributed to diagrammatic drawings of the Beetle, and an artist who simply signed his work SCHROEDER supplied a misty pastel interpretation of the factory, the four lift-outs included in "Der Volkswagen" were definitive early interpretations of each model. A real treasure was the cut-away image of the Beetle, populated by four people who appeared to have been drawn by another artist connected with the Volkswagen story, Victor Mundorff. The style was certainly his, and where Reuters appended his signature, a second hand added "+M". Admittedly, Mundorff normally signed work "VM", but the "M" here was in keeping with his hand.

Reuters opted to show the Standard model in profile and in this manner emphasised the curvy nature of the front and rear wings plus the metalwork surrounding the side windows. His elongation of the body was highlighted by masking the outline of the driver's door, while his clever choice of profile avoided presenting the boot lid of the base model and in so doing revealing its lack of trim and basic bumper-mounted horn. Similarly, the standard model's painted rather than chromed bumpers and hubcaps were not so obvious when looking at the side of the vehicle.

Perhaps inevitably, the Export model was angled to highlight its boot trim (including all-new Wolfsburg Crest badge) and abundance of chrome. Although the characteristics of a Reuters Beetle drawing were equally apparent, the rounded nature of the side windows, and in this instance the windscreen, were particularly noticeable.

To emphasise the main selling point of the sunroof model, Reuters tilted his subject towards the viewer. Apart from displaying the fold-back canvas sunroof (manufactured by Golde) to perfection, this angle brought the vehicle's interior into view. Few familiar with the thin and relatively Spartan nature of the Beetle's seat backrests would instantly recognise the luxuriously padded and amply proportioned luxury affairs created out of the artist's imagination.

Reuters's latest portrait of the Cabriolet, like that of the sunroof model, was carefully angled to portray the vehicle's soft-top and luxury rear-view window to best advantage. Like the drawing of the Cabriolet with its hood down, this image would be used and re-used time and time again.

DER VOLKSWAGEN

A second 1951 brochure carrying the title "Der Volkswagen". Reuters had only to produce artwork for the cover, as this publication re-used illustrations made for other Beetle and Transporter publications. Staying with the Beetle for the moment, each image was reduced to a grey-scale representation, but this was no black-and-white piece of print. While the cars and Transporter were presented thus, the background was offered in the mildest hue of pastel orange, with a bold line running across each page. The theme extended to other sheets of the 16-page brochure, which featured a combination of text, photography and illustrations of the Beetle (or Transporter) in a variety of locations and drawn by an unknown artist.

Reuters's cover depicted the export Beetle and Delivery Van with a front seat passenger and driver, but lacked the extremes of exaggeration so far apparent elsewhere.

Essentially, the Reuters Beetle story was up and running and, as will be discovered later, the artist was required to be much more prolific in respect of the Transporter. However, by the autumn of 1952 Reuters had to think again. The Beetle received its first serious makeover and so too did the format of the brochures to promote it.

DIE Sonnendach LIMOUSINE

A Matter of Continual improvement

October 1952 was a landmark in Nordhoff's policy of continual improvement. At the same time the format of Beetle brochures changed, being offered in a standard 210x297mm (A4) presentation and re-orientated to become portrait rather than landscape in shape. Inevitably, this orientation demanded additional artwork that gave scope to present the Beetle as large as possible on the page by driving it towards its observer. Reuters also opted to put people in all his new Beetles, and in one instance revisited an earlier drawing, tweaked it slightly and added a driver and passenger.

At first, as with the earliest brochure entitled "Meet the Volkswagen", the cover carried an incomplete outline of the Beetle, with a windswept lady behind the wheel and leaning out of the window. Reuters's most significant new artwork appeared on the inside front cover and as a centre spread. The latter included thumbnail interpretations of changes made in the October '52 makeover.

To coincide with the arrival of the Beetle with an oval-shaped rear window in March 1953, Reuters offered a new cover featuring the car previously occupying the centre spread of the late 1952 publication. He added an outline drawing of the Wolfsburg factory and one of his characteristic artistic lines. This look fronted all 10-page Beetle brochures until a difficult to determine point in 1956.

SEDAN
STANDARD AND DE LUXE MODELS

Do you like the European look in automobiles? Are you fond of clean-cut stream-lined cars? Are you keen on riding in easy comfort, yet would like to have a means of transportation that is downright cheap to operate? If such is the case, the Volkswagen, the leading European car in its field, is exactly what you are looking for. Technicians the world over say that the Volkswagen is the most sensible automobile ever built and that it is years ahead in design. The Volkswagen was designed by a genius as unique in his field as Caruso was as a tenor. The Volkswagen Sedan is built in two models, Standard and De Luxe. Both models are handsome in their shining metallic finish. The De Luxe Sedan offers a choice of bewitching colors. Expensive upholstery and handsome practical fittings blend into a harmonious whole with typical European discretion. All Volkswagen models offer the same basic features that make Volkswagens so outstanding. All have that surprisingly fast getaway, that smooth and safe driving thanks to marvelous suspension and a low center of gravity, and that extraordinary economy of operation combined with great driving comfort which characterize the Volkswagen and make it unequalled in its field.

The inside front cover carried brand new artwork, carefully designed to show a glimpse of the rear window, while also making the Beetle appear even longer, more roomy and airy than the offering of just a few months previously. Inevitably, Reuters re-coloured his cars to ensure successive reprints remained fresh and interesting to brochure browsers.

TEJADILHO MÓVEL

Right 1953 and below 1955 – care was taken to subtly update as fash-ions similarly moved forward.

Concurrent with the launch of the new 10-page brochure what might best be described as a deluxe publication also debuted. Totting up a total of 30 pages, including foldouts and tracing-style paper packed with information overlaying selected illustrations, its heavy-duty cover and pages were held together with a comb binder, a more upmarket arrangement than simple staples.

Initially the cover illustration was similar in nature to that of the late 1952 brochure discussed earlier, but from 1955 onwards, Reuters offered a much more lavish look (and one that was soon to be extended to the 10-page brochures as well). Comparable in nature to his more glamorous adverts and brochures produced for other manufacturers before the war, the initial offering depicted a De luxe Beetle descending a mountain pass while a sunroof model climbed effortlessly the other way. Note specifically how Reuters exaggerated the generosity this model's key selling point.

Interestingly, the design concept and artwork of these luxury brochures was attributed to Bernd Reuters by name.

The Bigger Picture

Just 12 months before his death Reuters's world was turned upside down, for Nordhoff sanctioned a further Beetle makeover. Every pane of glass on the car was larger – and in the case of the rear screen, by a massive 95 per cent. Reuters immediately broke an unwritten rule and turned the Beetle about, for the first time presenting the back of the car as the focal point of new cover artwork and the most significant inside page.

With considerable skill, the artist set his new work at night, thus highlighting the new rear window in the beam of an invisible streetlamp or, perhaps, the headlamps of another car. Light descended on the front-seat passenger and was even reflected through the rear view mirror but, with a degree of unavoidability, maximum emphasis was placed not only on the rear window but a lady looking towards the viewer. Note, too, how in place of what could have been simply a VW symbol dumped on the page, Reuters angled the famous roundel and made it the focal point of a shaft of light.

Such was the significance of the American market that Reuters was asked to add any extras in the specification specific to that market. Two-tier bumpers (designed to align with those on the average US saloon) were added in March 1955. Compare the US brochure cover on this page with the European market issue on the next.

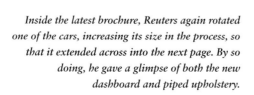

Inside the latest brochure, Reuters again rotated one of the cars, increasing its size in the process, so that it extended across into the next page. By so doing, he gave a glimpse of both the new dashboard and piped upholstery.

In 1958 Reuters made his new cover even more dramatic by changing the car's paintwork to what may have been his interpretation of a new shade, Diamond Grey. This allowed him to darken the hue of the night sky to a rich purple, probably the most spectacular shade ever to be portrayed on a VW brochure.

Theoretically his Beetle swansong, Reuters would have been glad to know that he went out on such a high.

BLICK INS INNERE

A View of the Interior

Brochures invariably included stylised dashboard imagery. Reuters's hand was clear to see in both the lower picture (post July 1957) and the earlier drawing (1953 onwards).

One for the ladies

Although the Cabriolet was included in most generic Beetle brochures, there were always publications dedicated to the top-of-the-range model. The probability is that Reuters's first work for Volkswagen was the Cabriolet brochure of 1950, which was re-issued over the next couple of years. Reuters made minor changes necessary to represent the car in its latest form, and at the same time resprayed the side panels of the car on the cover, altering the colour from burgundy to blue.

A brand new Cabriolet brochure was issued in 1954, and while the interior pages included a double-page spread of the car with its hood down (merely an updated version of the original artwork), the cover image was drawn specifically. Although instantly recognisable as Reuters's work, with characteristically chunkier tyres and beautifully polished paint and chrome, somehow the artist had managed to achieve a perfect look without his trademark tactic of elongating the vehicle and adding "speed lines". Even the sole occupant, the lady driver, couldn't be regarded as greatly out of scale to the proportions of the car.

The essence of the success of the drawing was that Reuters had dropped the hood and sculpted the driver's hair to flow behind her as she enjoyed the fresh air. That the driver was a woman, as in the earlier brochure, was no coincidence. Volkswagen's intention was undoubtedly to market the Cabriolet as a luxury version of the Beetle, suitable as a second car for affluent couples.

Reuters conjured up a new illustration for the cover for the 1958 model Cabriolet. Amazingly, he opted to raise the hood (although he wound down the side windows) and went back to elongating the car, adding "speed lines" and placing a decidedly small woman behind the wheel of a proportionately enormous car.

At first glance the 1957 image of the Cabriolet with its hood down appeared identical to that of earlier years. However Reuters had adapted his work to take into account the car's new engine lid, dashboard and even the inclusion of an external door mirror to the specification.

Although the new artwork of 1957 vintage survived through 1958, in 1959 the earlier cover artwork was restored. The colour of the car was changed to pink while items such as the door handles, sun-visors and interior rear-view mirror were updated to comply with the 1960 specification (available from August 1959).

An even greater shock was to follow in 1960 (for the 1961 model year). Reuters, already dead for two years, had apparently produced new artwork with a Cabriolet now facing to the right of the page, and with a man behind the wheel. The artwork is traceable back to the 1959 cover, but Reuters's signature had been removed. Another artist was updating the master's work.

Careful scrutiny soon reveals the right-facing car to be a mirror image of earlier left-facing vehicles. The most noticeable update – wing-mounted indicators – could easily have been snaffled from US-market artwork, where this style of flasher was in use before Reuters's death.

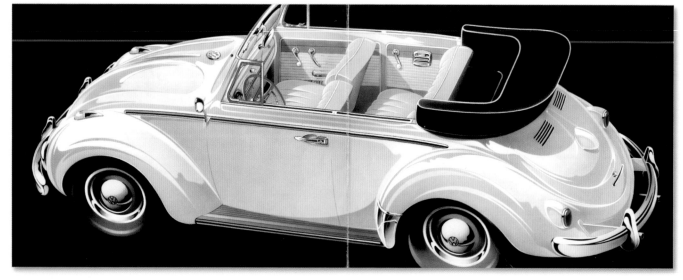

The appearance of the Cabriolet's interior for the 1961 model year brochure was transformed by a simple colour change. Models for all markets now carried wing-mounted front indicators.

With a little help from his friends

While the name Reuters epitomises Volkswagen's advertising during the 1950s, it isn't safe to assume everything came from his easel. Volkswagen's Transporter was taken out of Reuters's hands at some point towards the end of 1955 and handed over to the artist Robert Preis. Similarly, earlier brochures contained minor works from artists such as Schroeder who, for example, produced a series of thumbnail portraits for the brochure Der Kleinbus in 1951, or the even more anonymous "BV", who offered perfect miniatures for an untitled publication featuring Reuters's Transporter artwork.

One artist particularly worthy of mention is Viktor Mundorff, possibly best known in the field of transport for his work with Auto Union and NSU. Born in March 1897 in Bremen, he died in 1973; biographical details appear to suggest he was active between 1926 and 1964, and variously based in Chemitz, Ludwigsburg and Stuttgart.

His contributions to Volkswagen's advertising most notably included artwork for large showroom posters and series of postcards, originally used by dealers to notify customers of a due service or details of updated models. The posters, measuring 1195x795mm, were likely to portray, for example, the complete range of Beetles available. The poses were typically intended to convey the cars in action, and while clearly distinguishable as specific models they lacked the detail or exaggeration that characterised Reuters's style. This was even more evident in the postcards, the earliest of which appear to date from 1953 and feature the Ambulance, and in thumbnail sketches in some of the more elaborate Reuters-led brochures of the 1950s.

Mundorff was responsible for one brochure cover illustration during his years of work for Volkswagen, although during 1952 he prepared all the artwork for a small 12-page portrait-shape publication devoted to a Cabriolet's journey. Three small watercolours portrayed the car making its way through the autumn and winter landscape, while a fourth showed it having reached its destination. Despite one illustration being set in snow and another suggesting chilly conditions, the Cabriolet's hood was firmly set for open-air motoring.

Mundorff's work finally achieved cover status in 1959. Such was its impact that Volkswagen clearly thought it unnecessary to add a title or even the famous VW roundel.

Mundorff's elevation to brochure cover status came as late as 1959, towards the end of the period when artwork dominated Volkswagen's advertising. In an untitled 16-page landscape publication, Mundorff not only contributed the cover, but also ten additional illustrations, two of which were of more than thumbnail size. The cover depicted a Micro Bus De Luxe in the foreground and a Micro Bus in the middle distance, set against a backdrop of an ornate promenade and a clear blue sea. The other illustrations depicted the same two vehicles among other settings. After page five no further examples of Mundorff's work appeared, with more detailed illustrations by Robert Preis taking over. These illustrated the finer points of each vehicle, which demonstrated Mundorff's place in the advertising story as a scene setter whose work was closer to the landscapes adorned the walls of a family home than any of his contemporaries.

Illustrations from the internal pages of Mundorff's 1959 brochure.

The all-weather bus off to winter sports.

Station Wagon ... especially during hours or on runs where the passenger load is small. Hotel managements, resorts, airlines, travel services all over the world are enthusiastic users of these Station Wagons. Their distinctive appearance, and comfort, make them ideal for economical shuttle transportation, trips and sightseeing tours for guests who enjoy the best.

In the U.S.A., the Station Wagon is a familiar sight everywhere.

Ideal for camping and family trips.

Precision built by the finest automated machinery and finished with traditional German craftsmanship, the Station Wagon offers you honest value in performance and quality. Its popularity has been so terrific that Volkswagen was obliged to build a brand-new factory in Hannover to keep abreast of its customers requirements.
The Volkswagen Station Wagon is at home on all continents. The sturdy air-cooled Volkswagen engine functions dependably under the sub-zero climate of the Alaskan Tundra or in the hot sands of the Sahara.

The VW Station Wagon is a dependable vehicle for trips anywhere in the world.

Always in time for school.

The De Luxe Station Wagon — a favorite for airport shuttle service.

1952 – four watercolours by Mundorff from the small-format Cabriolet brochure "Fahre gesund unt mit Genuss."

Mundorff's artwork featured on a series of dealer publicity postcards throughout the 1950s. Even the Karmann Ghia (below centre) was handed over to his skills although specification detail was far from clear.

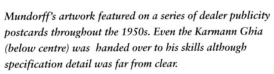

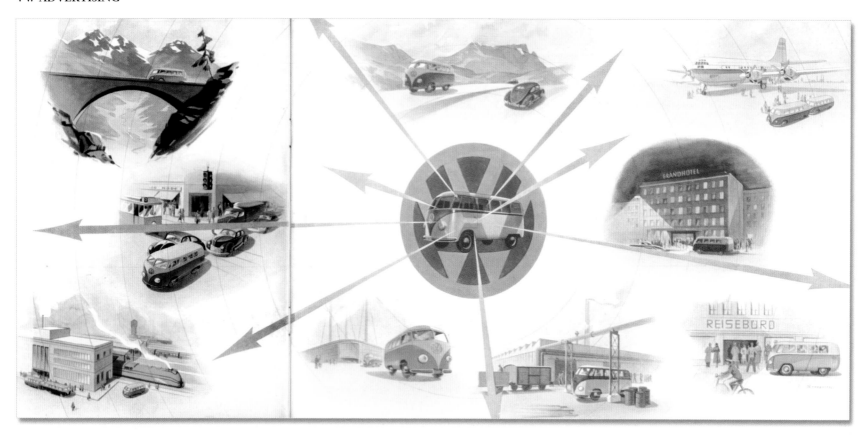

The series of thumbnail style illustrations (above), which appeared in the two deluxe brochures entitled "Der Kleinbus", both published in 1951, were the work of the artist Schroeder.

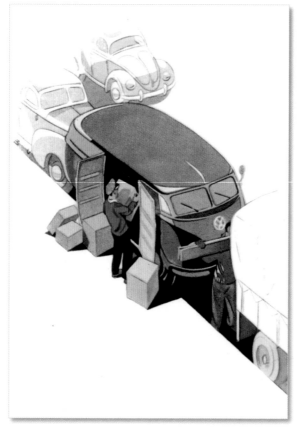

Dating from the same year and included in an untitled Transporter brochure is the distinctly anonymous work of BV.

Fashion Photography

Even though 1950s' fashion was for stylised interpretations of the range through the skills of artists, photography played its part in Volkswagen's promotional material. Presented in chronological order, here is a gallery of the finest.

Standard-model Beetle bringing up the rear, while the De Luxe and Cabriolet flank the Micro Bus, which has been finished in a bespoke colour scheme. ("Der Kleinbus" version one, July 1951)

Ladies dressed for an occasion were clearly impressed by the mirror-gloss paintwork. ("Der Volkswagen", 1951).

Eight people and 11 cases – the worlds' first genuine people carrier. If only the adjoining photo was in colour – the original Volkswagen Christmas card! ("Der Kleinbus", July 1951).

The purpose of this brochure was undoubtedly to launch the De Luxe version of the Micro Bus. The fold-back sunroof and abundance of light, airy window glass were key themes (later "Der Kleinbus" brochure, October 1951).

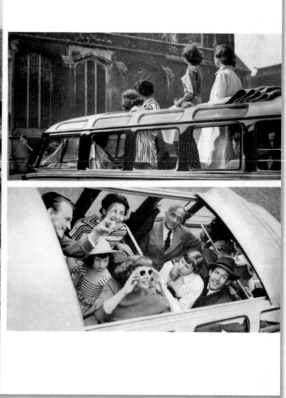

Photography designed to sell a story, in this instance one of the luxury and aspirations associated with ownership of the De Luxe Beetle. Taken from a brochure issued in 1952 and entitled "Volkswagen presents its products".

A rare glimpse of Volkswagen's stand at a motor show ("Volkswagen Presents Its Products", 1952).

For the grand tour ("Volkswagen Presents Its Products", 1952).

A picnic for eight – not to mention the little boy ("Volkswagen Presents Its Products", 1952).

Another take on the carrying abilities of the Micro Bus ("VW Micro Bus", 1953).

Presenting the full cover story (from the 1954 brochure "VW Cabriolet", proof that there was life outside the world of Reuters).

Demonstrating that the Delivery Van could carry a
substantial load, while also illustrating that the lack
of rear access made the task more difficult
("VW Kastenwagen", 1954).

Reuters couldn't resist adding
"speed lines" to make this
Beetle go faster (untitled 30-
page Beetle brochure, 1955).

A rarity, as this is one of less than
a handful of images to depict the
US Beetle of 1955 with its new
bullet-style indicators and two-
tier bumpers (untitled US-market
brochure, 1955).

Words, Words, Words

Generally, brochure text was overly wordy and somewhat ponderous in style. Such a statement might well be applicable to the output of all 1950s carmakers; it is certainly true of Volkswagen's literature, as the following examples illustrate.

On introducing the Beetle to the British market in 1953:

"Do you like the European look in automobiles? Are you fond of clean-cut streamlines? Do you like to ride in easy comfort, yet would like to have a means of transport that is downright cheap to operate? If such is the case, the Volkswagen, the leading European car in its field, is exactly what you are looking for. Technicians the world over say that the Volkswagen is the most sensible automobile ever built and that it is years ahead in design. The Volkswagen was designed by a genius as unique in his field as Caruso was as a tenor…"

The car for a lady – the Convertible, circa 1953:

"If you like to drive a sporty car and enjoy sunshine to the full, the Volkswagen Convertible is the car for you. Wherever you drive or park a Volkswagen Convertible, it attracts the admiring attention of all eyes. Volkswagen has built in the Convertible the car of your dreams. Like all other Volkswagen models, the Convertible has no wasted space or superfluous weight. Not an inch of space is unused and every ounce of weight is put to good use. The Convertible is the fastest and easiest handling car in turbulent city traffic. Put the top up on a Convertible and you can drive through a cloudburst in comfort. It is absolutely impervious to rain, wind, dust and cloud. It is hard to talk a woman into a Sedan when she has seen the graceful lines of the Convertible (body by Karmann)."

The Delivery Van pitch for the gullible employer, circa 1954:

"Think of your drivers. If you want them to cut down delivery costs for you, give them vehicles they enjoy using. It will please them to have something special, particularly when it saves them so much work. Notice how roomy the cab is. It seats three as comfortably as on a sofa. Heating and wing ventilators are standard equipment. Large doors afford easy access. There is no danger of soiling your clothes when getting in and out in bad weather as the open doors shield them from any part of the vehicle they might brush against. It is relaxing to drive a Volkswagen Transporter. The steering wheel is convenient to the hand and steering is a pleasure.

"Like a pilot in his cockpit, the driver has all-round vision and also has a close-up view of the road right up to the front of the vehicle. This as well as the amazing Volkswagen get-away is one of the reasons why Volkswagen Transporters are so remarkably fast in city traffic."

The Honest Car, an introduction to the 1958 model year Beetle, a seven-paragraph statement including a policy directive from the office of Heinz Nordhoff:

"In ten short years the Volkswagen has risen from total obscurity to become a household name on every continent, an accepted international yardstick for judging an automobile. Of all the cars exported in the world, the Volkswagen now holds undisputed first place.

"The Volkswagen has an ideal sales force: some two million happy owners. No wonder the constantly increasing output at Wolfsburg never catches up with the demand.

"Why is it that the imagination of two million Volkswagen owners has been fired by this amazing car?

"Because it possesses a combination of performance and economy never before known in automobile design.

"Because of its sensible engineering and sturdy construction. Because it does not pretend to be anything but what it is – an honest car.

"Because there has been a consistent policy, not swayed by the whims of fashion, holding fast to what has proved itself, yet constantly improving the car and so raising it to an internationally admired pitch of perfection."

The Box on Wheels Needs Help

Although Reuters's association with the Transporter didn't last to the end of his life, his output was prolific. Conceivably, as the Beetle more-or-less sold itself, and with demand outstripping supply, Nordhoff could well have asked the artist to spend more time on the second string to Volkswagen's bow. Although production figures don't necessarily support such claims, more than one VW historian has suggested that, at least in the early days, the Transporter wasn't the rip-roaring success that had been predicted. Reuters was the ideal candidate to assist with reversing of any sign of ill fortune.

Apart from the generic *Der Volkswagen*, Reuters produced no less than five covers and a wealth of secondary images during 1951. Two of them, both destined to be short-lived in exposure, ranked high among Reuters's finest, while a second duo (see Family Matters, page 48) were destined to be the forerunners of a set covering every main variation on the Transporter theme. The fifth, but not the last to be released, offered an introduction to the core model Delivery Van, plus a glimpse of the Transporter's role as a passenger carrier, and would remain in the showrooms throughout 1951 and at least part way into 1952.

DAS TRANSPORTER-PROGRAMM FÜR PERSONENBEFÖRDERUNG UND GÜTERTRANSPORT

Dedicated solely to the VW Transporter, this 1951 brochure was presented in landscape format (measuring a nominal 290x200mm); with the exception of the front cover, each page carried a fold-out flap that added 146x200mm to the overall size. The centre spread was dedicated to these docile drawings portraying the Delivery Van, and a side-on representation of the Kombi ("Das Transporter-programm für Personenbeförderung und Gütertransport" or "The Transporter range for passengers and the carrying of goods"). Reuters's artwork was tame, in that the vehicle's lines were not really exaggerated, there were no proportionately too-small passengers, no dramatic backgrounds and no indication of movement; indeed the side view was little more than two-dimensional.

The cover of the 1951 Transporter brochure was much more inspirational than some of the internal pages. Reuters set the stage for future illustrations by angling his work to portray the Transporter from a sitting or crouching position, and in so doing accentuated its distinctive front and split screen. Three occupants were sitting some distance from each other in typically disproportionate manner, while the "speed lines" clearly conveyed the message of a vehicle hurtling towards its destination. At the rear, Reuters sculptured a curvy vehicle far removed from the concept of a utilitarian box on wheels.

The National Portrait Gallery – Artwork fit to be hung in a premiere exhibition

Production of "Der Kleinbus" (also known as "Der VW Achtsitzer" or the "Micro Bus") had started as early as May 1950, and 1142 examples had left Wolfsburg by the end of the year. But it wasn't until 1951 that the fully-fledged people carrier acquired its own dedicated and luxurious 12-page brochure. To mark the occasion, Reuters produced a stunning cover image, as well as sketching a delightful duo of Micro Buses (one complete and the other in cutaway form) for the centrefold.

For once, the artist portrayed his stylised vehicle in standard colours, no doubt confirming his admiration for the aesthetics of rich Chestnut Brown over sophisticated Sealing Wax Red. Otherwise, every aspect of the work showed Reuters at his classic best: accentuated curves, unrealistically spacious cab (thanks to disproportionately small passengers), a low down angle to create a more impressive look, "speed lines" and a great outdoors setting.

The French language version (left) of the first "Der Kleinbus" brochure lacked a title, Volkswagen instead relying on the selling power of the famous VW roundel alone.

Production of a De Luxe version of the already well-appointed Micro Bus started on 1 June 1951. It was marketed in Germany as Der VW Kleinbus Sonderausführung (special edition). Reuters produced an even more stunning cover for a revised and enlarged 16-page version of the Kleinbus brochure, while the selection of photographs in this image-led publication was similarly updated to take into account the attributes of the latest model.

Reuters made his all-adventure backdrop even more stunning, ensured the occupants of his new vehicle sat away from the windscreen and each other (creating an even greater impression of space) and presented a sunroof so generous in proportions that sceptics might well have questioned the vehicle's structural safety. Like the woman sitting on the rear seat, browsers could virtually breathe the Alpine air.

Hot on the heels of "Der Kleinbus" featuring the Micro Bus De Luxe, Reuters produced a third classic. Logically, this latest artwork should have been made available for all to see in 1951, yet despite the artist dating his work to that year, the first brochure to feature the new cover image appears to date from January 1952. While Reuters's Delivery Van loomed towards the beholder (positioned so low that parts of the undercarriage were plain to see), a Kombi, or Micro Bus, sped past in the opposite direction, thus revealing its rear window (a new standard feature from April 1951). No doubt with the Delivery Van in mind, Reuters placed his vehicles in a city environment, a street bustling with traffic, set against contemporary high-rise apartments and offices.

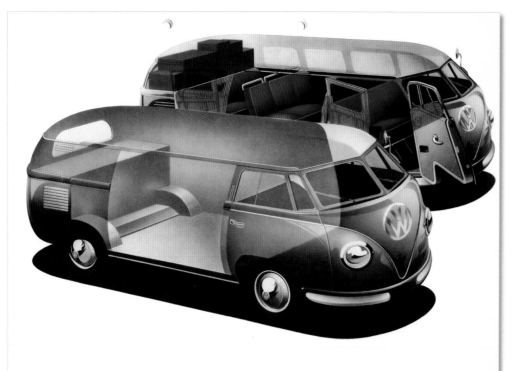

The interior pages of the January 1952 brochure "Die VW Transporter" included the remarkable cutaway Micro Bus (of "Der Kleinbus" fame) which was now joined by a Delivery Van finished in ubiquitous Dove Blue. Designed to emphasise the space available for crates, boxes and every other conceivable object, to today's eyes it also accentuates the intrusive nature of the engine compartment. Surprisingly, the page on which this appeared was totally devoid of text.

More visual appeal came from sketches placed on the extremities of main text sheets. The Delivery Van was shown parked as a Beetle passed by, its driver loading boxes and a barrel under the ever-watchful eye of a supervisor. Meanwhile, people (including a chauffeur complete with uniform and hat) prepared to board a hotel's courtesy Micro Bus. The style of the unsigned works was not overtly that of Reuters and may come from the hand of the mysterious BV, one of the artists who supplemented his work.

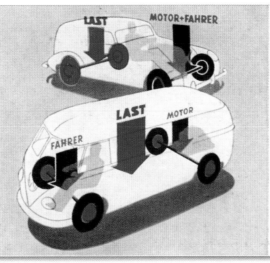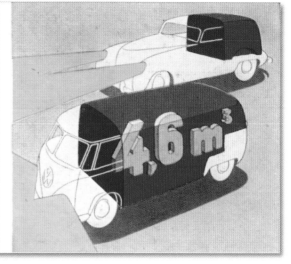

Small sketches (not necessarily by Reuters) soon became standard material in Delivery Van brochures. Each compared the Transporter to standard vans of the times, indicating, in sequence, the greater acreage of plain metal available to promote a business (Grosse Werbefläche, large advertising space), the ideal counterbalancing arrangement of driver at the front, engine at the rear and load between, plus finally the significance of a much larger carrying capacity than average..

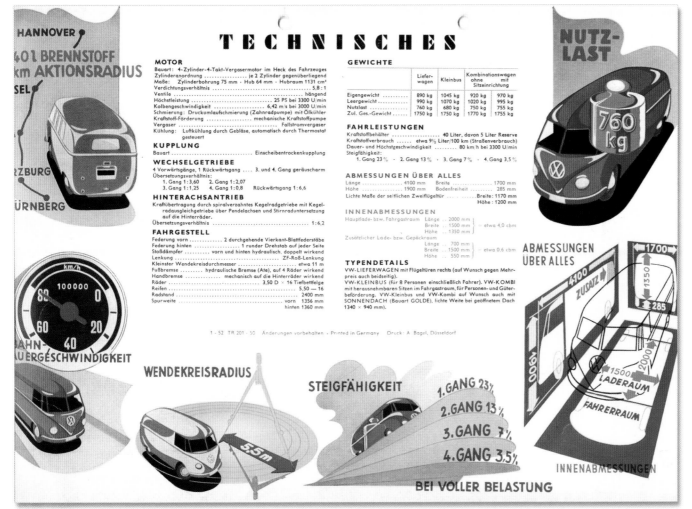

Delightfully, Reuters offered a repeat of the treat he prepared for the back page of the later (October 1951) "Der Kleinbus" publication. Five thumbnail sketches advised that with 40 litres of fuel in a full tank, 430 kilometres of road stretched before the Transporter driver, while on the Autobahn the cruising speed was a fast-and-furious 80kph. With the aid of a giant protractor, Reuters carefully calculated that the Transporter's turning circle radius was no more than 5.5 metres, while, when the vehicle was fully laden, he indicated what gradients could be accomplished.

Family Matters

The Transporter was planned from the outset as a vehicle open to a multitude of uses, and Director General Nordhoff designed a rolling programme of Transporter model introductions. When Reuters's name appeared, the Delivery Van, Kombi and Micro Bus were already in steady production. During 1951, these models were joined by the Micro Bus De Luxe and, perhaps the most unusual mainstream model of them all, the niche-market Ambulance. 1952 would see the debut of the Pick-up. Reuters's task was to produce recognisably compatible artwork suitable for the covers of a series of four page model specific brochures. As the four-page brochures were destined to stay in print with revisions until some point in

VW-KLEINBUS „SONDERAUSFÜHRUNG"

The earliest print run of the 285 x 210mm four page brochure "VW-Kleinbus Sonderausführung" appears to date from September 1951 and as such slightly predates the second of the lavish multi-page Der Kleinbus publications. Inevitably the text is abridged by comparison, while the number of photos and illustrations are similarly reduced although, of course, only one type of Micro Bus, rather than two, is featured.

Reuters's artwork was intentionally more conservative, lacking the background atmosphere of the other Kleinbus brochures, but he still carefully implied a more curvaceous nose at the vehicle's front, rescaled its occupants and added wisps of go-faster lines. Interestingly, as would become standard in the forthcoming series of four-page brochures, he adopted the viewpoint most advantageous to the specific model. Thus he angled the vehicle so that the observer looked down towards the De Luxe, and in so doing could view its canvas roof, which would have been virtually impossible from most angles. He left the fold-back roof closed, but by opting for this position revealed the four Plexiglas skylights unique to the top-of-the-range model. He managed to retain the curvy look, accentuated the crease in the roofline above the split panes of the windscreen – not possible elsewhere – and revealed the luggage area above the engine, complete with shiny rails to protect the glass.

1955, Reuters updated his drawings, either to illustrate the vehicle's latest features, or simply to offer a fresh look.

Having created a cover image for the new Ambulance (launched at the end of 1951 and outlined in detail on page 67), Reuters quickly produced artwork for the existing models, the Delivery Van, VW Kombi and VW Kleinbus. In this last instance, Volkswagen marketing gurus appear to have thought the term Kleinbus, literally 'small bus', lacking and soon suggested the title of VW-Achtsitzer, or eight-seater. Inevitably, the four-page Pick-up brochure was already designed and in print when the model was launched on 25 August 1952.

From March 1955, all Transporters sported a different roofline amongst other significant but less visual changes The longer term implications of this re-design and the way Reuters interpreted it are discussed on page 58, but examples are illustrated on forthcoming pages.

Between publication of the original Micro Bus De Luxe brochure and the one reproduced here (dated February 1953), Reuters gave the vehicle a respray to more palatable, but still non-standard, colours. He also changed the angle of the wing mirror from an upward to downward fixing (July 1952) and opened the quarter-light to illustrate its pivoting action (which had replaced the piano-hinge style at the beginning of 1953).

VW-Achtsitzer „Sondermodell"

VW-LIEFERWAGEN

IMPORT:
PON's AUTOMOBIELHANDEL N.V.
Arnhemseweg 2-14   **AMERSFOORT**   Telefoon 6545 (6 lijnen)

Reuters decided that the most important feature of the Delivery Van was its substantial load space, coupled to its safety-conscious, side-loading doors. His side profile ensured both were seen to best advantage. The closed quarter-light evident in the image above confirms the cover's early status (February 1952). Brochures dating from the start of 1953 and later showed an open quarter-light, the result of a redesign by Volkswagen to pivoting hinges.

In the version dating from 1955 (right), the peak above the split-pane windscreen was the most obvious change. However, the eagle-eyed will spot an increase in the size of the three load area vents, the addition of a ninth air intake to the engine compartment, the relocation of the petrol filler flap to a position close to the vents, the addition of a rear bumper and a change in style of the opening mechanism for the side-loading doors.

VW-Kastenwagen

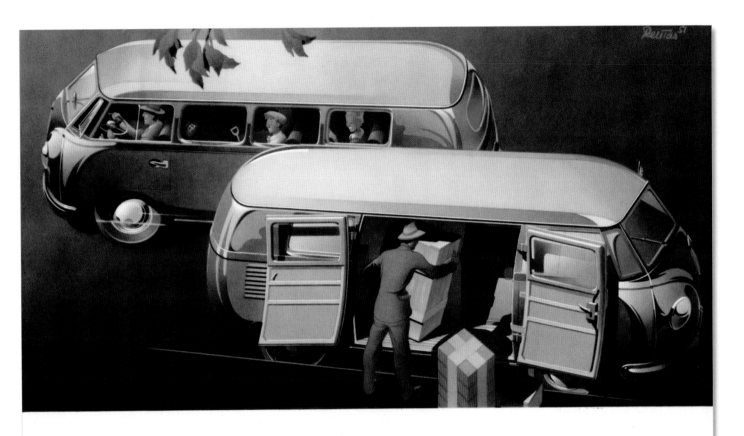

VW-Kombi

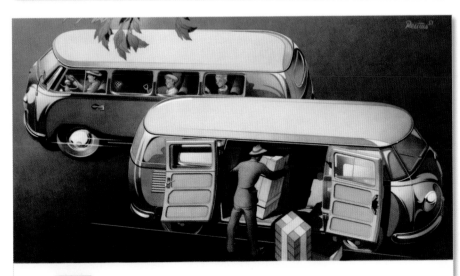

VW-Kombi

Whereas it was important to stress the capacity of the Delivery Van by portraying the acreage of plain metal to best advantage, in the case of the Kombi it was wiser to open the side-loading doors when the vehicle was in van mode, with the purpose of illustrating the interior without seats. In both guises Reuters exaggerated available space. Note the space between the generously proportioned loading doors and, particularly, the distance between the driver and the first row of passengers when the Kombi was shown in passenger-carrying guise.

Comparing roof panels between the earlier (1953, above) and later (1955, left) versions, the illusion of a heavy snowfall afflicting the newer Kombi, or, more disarmingly, the application of a thick layer of royal icing, is very apparent.

VW-Kleinbus

VW-Achtsitzer

The final version (above right, 1955) of Reuters's four-page Micro Bus brochure illustrates identical changes to those already described for the Delivery Van with the sole exception of the side-loading door handle. The early version (above, 1952) was released in the days of the piano hinge style quarter-light so Reuters opted to keep the window closed.

What is more noteworthy is Reuters's persistence in portraying his vehicles in non-standard colours. Vehicles finished only in primer remained important to Volkswagen throughout the 1950s. If Reuters had opted to represent his Micro Bus in official colours, his choice for the 1952 version would have been between either Stone Grey and or Brown Beige upper panels over a Light Beige lower body.

Like the Ambulance before it, the Pick-up's important feature was its load bed. Reuters turned the vehicle accordingly. Cleverly, he also depicted the Pick-up from the passenger side, in the process revealing another key selling point, the under-bed secure storage area (carefully loaded with the more valuable items). While the artist subtly extended the proportions of the load bed, he could do little with the men unloading the vehicle. To make them disproportionately small would have been to deny the Pick-up one of its greatest selling points, namely a loading platform at an ideal height. Reuters was particularly clever to show one of his two workers lowering the tailgate, while the other had clearly already dropped the side gate. Between the two brochures, pre- and post-March 1955, the appearance of a rear bumper was obvious and the cab peak readily detectable. More significant in terms of robustness were the reinforcing mouldings on the gates, something Reuters was quick to include in revised drawings completed after 11 November 1953. (1953 below left, 1955 below)

VW-Pritschenwagen
„Pick-up"

VW-Pritschenwagen „Pick-up"

Selling Space

At first glance, Reuters appeared to have produced a further cover image for another Transporter brochure of 1951 vintage. "Wer fährt VW Transporter?" (Who drives the VW Transporter?) was designed to promote the advantage of the Delivery Van's versatility as a promotional billboard. Sales of Transporters finished in primer were extremely promising, but in the act of producing a brochure devoted entirely to liveried Delivery Vans, Kombis and even Micro Buses, Volkswagen offered a gentle reminder that the new vehicle was a source of free advertising.

Extending to 24 text-free pages, this large (295x210mm) brochure illustrated no less than 86 liveried examples of the Transporter. Of particular interest was the image on the inside front cover, for this depicted the first Delivery Van to be sold, a vehicle bearing the chassis number 000014, which had been finished in primer when delivered to the Autohaus Fleischhauer in Cologne on 8 March 1950. The dealer's customer was the 4711 Perfume Company, whose intention it was to have the vehicle adorned with both the company logo and its house colours.

Reuters's contribution to this brochure was minimal. The artwork on the cover wasn't new, as it was simply a cropped greyscale version of the work produced for the front of his recent Transporter brochure. Clearly, the format worked, for within less than a year a new, greatly enlarged version of the brochure made its debut.

"*Wer Fährt VW Transporter?*" version two appeared in dealers' show-rooms in summer 1952. The page count had bounced up to 54 from 24, the proportion of vehicles portrayed in full-colour had increased dramatically, and there was a greater feeling that the publication had been mteticulously designed rather than casually strung together. Now, for example, vehicles sporting the logos of various airlines were portrayed against the background of the latest aeroplanes. Similarly, Transporters owned by newspaper companies were depicted against a background of broadsheet titles, while the design also included the use of sepia tints.

Despite the size of the brochure (which featured 168 liveried vehicles), text remained virtually non-existent. The English version simply suggested that browsers should, "Please design your own advertising to suit your taste". Perforated pull-out pages allotted to a front, rear and side-view outline of the Transporter were provided to assist customers to complete Volkswagen's request.

Volkswagen's general attention to detail is evident in their request to Reuters to design a new cover for this latest version of "*Wer Fährt VW Transporter?*" The resultant artwork possibly made the cab of the Transporter look even more impressive, but essentially all the familiar traits were simply rehashed: the low angle, exceptionally glossy paint-work, and the cab's diminutive occupants.

Working with Special Models

Lacking artwork by Reuters or his fellow artists instead the brochure aptly relied on photography and clever, familiar background designs throughout. As early as 1951, Transporter parts manuals included what was listed as SP equipment (Sonderpackung). Having described and illustrated a variety of special models in the in-house magazine *VW Information*, in 1954 (initially for the home market only), Volkswagen produced a brochure illustrating a wide range. It was entitled "VW Transporter zweckvolle Inneneinrichtungen" and in 1956 a multilingual version rendered the English language title as "Interior equipment for Volkswagen Transporters".

It contained no work by Reuters or any of his fellow artists, instead relying on photography and clever, but largely familiar, background design throughout. No fewer than 44 models, sometimes in several poses, were depicted in the 50-page 295x210mm landscape brochure. These ranged through mobile shops, bread vans, livestock transporters, mobile offices and workshops, airport fuelling and aeroplane 'follow-me' vehicles, mobile kitchens and exhibition vans.

Text was limited, but for those in search of an unusual Volkswagen to use for a special purpose, rewarding.

"You can see how ingeniously the VW Delivery Van can be equipped for practical purposes. You can see the VW Pick-up with a closed-in body for the delivery of meat and sausages.

"Interior equipment for Volkswagen Transporters" (1956 version, multilingual text).

Drinks Pick-up and Delivery Van.

Police Mobile Incident Room.

Roof platform and special option full-width dashboard.

You can see them as milk trucks, stock display trucks or even as mobile workshops. The VW Kombi is shown as training vehicle, radio interference tracker and publicity car. And finally you can see the VW Eight-Passenger Standard and De Luxe Micro Bus models used for travelling, hunting and camping trips and as television car."

This early brochure was a near contemporary of more specialist publications, such as the 1956 leaflet dedicated to the "VW Feuerlöschfahrzeug" (VW Fire Pump). In 1958 came a lengthy series of single-sided sheets, each devoted to a specific special-purpose model and all following the same design and size. They were replaced later in the year with an equally extensive string of 285x210mm double-sided leaflets dedicated to the same series of vehicles. However, each now carried an SO number – the example featured is the "VW-Verkaufswagen" (Mobile Shop), which was SO1. Without detouring too far into Transporter specification territory, the initials SO stood for Sonderausführungen, or literally "special designs". During this period, Volkswagen had formalised the special body market, allocating SO numbers to officially licensed body builders.

Initially, SO designations also carried the name of the location where the body builder was based. Dealers might have opted to include a rather dull brochure (or more realistically, pamphlet) covering a selection of the special models when handing out a folder containing individual publications detailing the mainstream models. Essentially a black-and-white production with spot-colour blue added, the four-page 210x298mm leaflet was text heavy and out of keeping with Volkswagen's usual publicity material. However, it served its purpose, even reminding customers that the Transporter could be specified as a camper – "VW Transporter mit Wohneinrichtung" (VW Transporter with Living Equipment), SO22 and SO23.

Single sheet, special model publication "VW Refrigerator Van with Compressor"', 1959.

"VW Verkaufswagen (SO1)" (Mobile Shop), 1958.

"VW Transporter Sonderaufbauten", 1956/7.

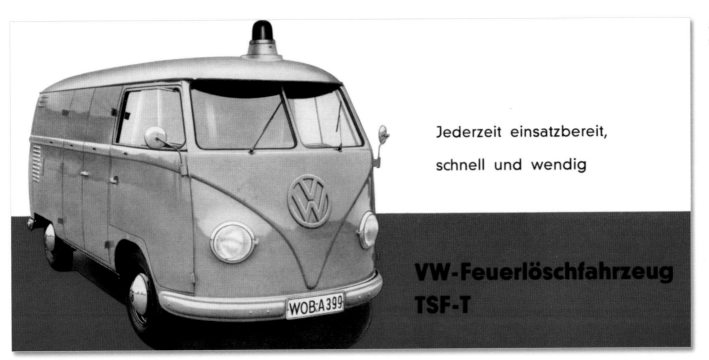

Jederzeit einsatzbereit,

schnell und wendig

**VW-Feuerlöschfahrzeug
TSF-T**

*Small-format fire ancillary
vehicle brochure, 1956*

**Volkswagen-
Transporter
im Winterdienst**

mit Federschneepflug und
elektrischem Kleinstreuer
zum Räumen und Streuen von
Radfahrwegen – Parkplätzen,
Fabrikhöfen, Gartenanlagen und
Fußgängerwegen

Schneller und leichter Anbau, sofort
einsatzfähig

Schneepflug:
links- und rechtsräumend
Ölhydraulische Heb- und Senkvorrichtung
vom Führerhaus aus bedienbar
volle Ausweichmöglichkeit bei
Hindernissen

Elektrischer Kleinstreuer:
wird mit Bosch-Motor 6- oder 12-Volt aus-
gerüstet. Streubreite durch Schiebewider-
stand einstellbar.
In Kommunalbetrieben und Straßenbau-
ämtern seit Jahren tausendfach bewährt.

Nutzen Sie Ihre Volkswagen-Transporter
auch im Winterdienst. Die Anschaffung von
Spezialfahrzeugen erübrigt sich.
Sie sparen Geld und können ihre Transporter mit diesen Zusatzgeräten schnell
und billig ausrüsten.

*"VW Transporter im
Winterdienst", circa 1963.*

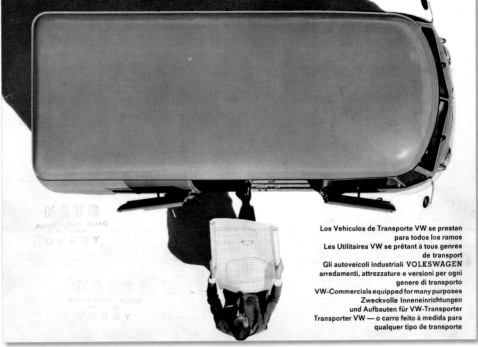

Los Vehiculos de Transporte VW se prestan
para todos los ramos
Les Utilitaires VW se prêtant à tous genres
de transport
Gli autoveicoli industriali VOLKSWAGEN
arredamenti, attrezzature e versioni per ogni
genere di transporto
VW-Commercials equipped for many purposes
Zweckvolle Inneneinrichtungen
und Aufbauten für VW-Transporter
Transporter VW — o carro feito à medida para
qualquer tipo de transporte

*Emphasising the importance of special models in 1962, a
further full-scale brochure, again of a multilingual style, was
offered. "VW Commercials equipped for many purposes",
extended to 32 pages and was essentially an updated version
of the 1955/6 brochure, and even included imagery from the
original. However, the 'by association' backgrounds had
disappeared, while the unusual cover angle was probably its
most striking feature.*

57

Reuters Leaves a Blot

When Reuters amended his series of model-specific Transporter drawings to accommodate the revised roofline of March 1955, most artwork was recycled in preference to starting from scratch.

Unfortunately, given a blank canvas, the result was less appealing than previous work, and proved to be Reuters's last as far as the Transporter was concerned.

Here, Reuters depicted a Micro Bus and a Delivery Van in apparently mountainous territory, as both front ends were tilted upwards to expose the new roofline. His skill at believable exaggeration, most notably spaciousness for the vehicles' occupants and exceptionally glossy paintwork panels, was still apparent, but let down by a windscreen peak that was ugly and implausible.

Volkswagen had spent a fortune retooling for a much smaller engine compartment, coupled to rear loading access. Reuters's third vehicle could have portrayed these improvements, but instead the artist opted to show the one model to which they did not apply.

Perhaps the saving grace of Reuters's 1955 brochure artwork was that the interior pages relied on a combination of photography and what looked suspiciously like the unsigned work of Preis, the man soon to be responsible for official artistic interpretation of the Transporter.

Preis Takes the Transporter on Board

Within 12 months of the Transporter's 1955 revamp, artist Robert Preis had not only reworked the cover image of Reuters's final brochure for the range, but had also skilfully updated model-specific literature. Essentially, the two cover images – one by Reuters and the other by Preis – mirrored each other in appearance, the new work being at first glance little more than a pastiche of the old. Preis's Micro Bus wore the same combination of paint colours as his predecessor's (the vehicle's official tones of Palm Green over Sand Green), and both Delivery Vans were finished in a red hue, an option that didn't become standard until the summer of 1958. Similarly, both artists featured a Pick-up in the mid-distance.

However, while Preis's style was less extravagant and lacked the eye-catching exuberance of Reuters on form, in this instance his conservatism paid off. Both his Delivery Van and Micro Bus appeared less like caricatures of the latest Transporters, the gross nature of Reuters's peaked roofs being replaced with something sufficiently close to reality to be convincing.

Dutifully Preis followed in the footsteps of the master. He reduced the size of drivers and passengers in proportion to that of the vehicles, just as he likewise attempted to make his paintwork gleam. He even sank to his knees to obtain the finest perspective of the Delivery Van. Better still, though, was his Pick-up, as he had opted to reverse it a little in order to show the full cab properly.

From this promising starting point, the largely unknown Robert Preis scored with new poses and clever adaptations of Reuters's work to such an extent that he was to be more or less responsible for Volkswagen's Transporter literature for the rest of the decade.

The new-for-1956 generic Transporter material, either in the form of a folder holding individual model brochures, or as a piece of literature knitting the core range into one, contained illustrations and descriptions of the key updates of the 1955 makeover.

With a little help from his friends, Preis illustrated the new full-length dashboard (previously exclusive to the Micro Bus De Luxe) and the all-important rear hatch (using the technique of an outline drawing, with full colour inserts where it really mattered).

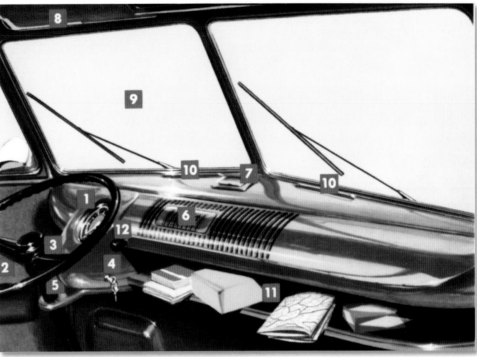

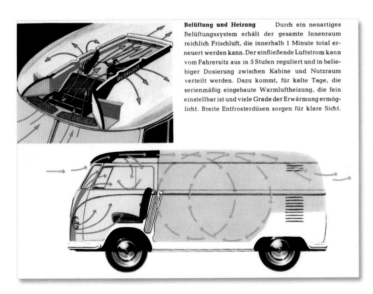

Mimicking what Reuters had created, Preis offered cutaway illustrations of the Micro Bus De Luxe and Delivery Van, updated thumbnails covering advertising space and weight distribution, and presenting new interpretations in a similar format encompassing cruising and hill-climbing abilities, as well as fuel economy and manoeuvrability.

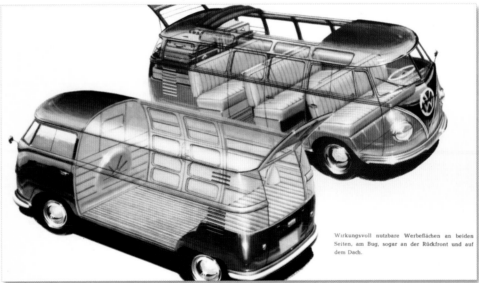

Wirkungsvoll nutzbare Werbeflächen an beiden Seiten, am Bug, sogar an der Rückfront und auf dem Dach.

Belüftung und Heizung Durch ein neuartiges Belüftungssystem erhält der gesamte Innenraum reichlich Frischluft, die innerhalb 1 Minute total erneuert werden kann. Der einfließende Luftstrom kann vom Fahrersitz aus in 5 Stufen reguliert und in beliebiger Dosierung zwischen Kabine und Nutzraum verteilt werden. Dazu kommt, für kalte Tage, die serienmäßig eingebaute Warmluftheizung, die fein einstellbar ist und viele Grade der Erwärmung ermöglicht. Breite Entfrosterdüsen sorgen für klare Sicht.

Preis produced explanatory sketches of the innovatory air-circulation system, without resorting to exaggerating the revised roof peak.

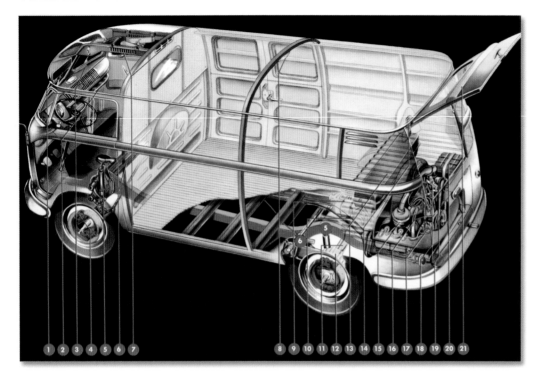

The new folder and generic Transporter brochures included this delightful cutaway drawing, material reminiscent of the work of earlier days, but dutifully updated to illustrate fully all the vehicle's latest features. An accompanying key to the main features accumulated 21 separate points worthy of mention.

VW-Kastenwagen

Preis recognised that Reuters's side view of the Delivery Van, which was intended to exaggerate its already generous length, no longer represented what was really required. As a result, he turned the vehicle so that key elements of the design were on view. One man could be seen loading lengthy tubes through the new hatch, while the driver manhandled a crate through the side door. By opening the side-loading doors, Preis could illustrate how easily the most awkward of boxes slipped into the van.

VW-Kombi

VW-Pritschenwagen „Pick-up"

For the Pick-up, Preis retained the Reuters pose but dropped one side-gate and the tailgate. This allowed browsers to have a clear view of the load bed and its hardwood rails. Through clever use of perspective, Preis managed to both depict the real length of the Pick-up's bed, and exaggerate its proportions in relation to the size of the less important cab area.

Preis produced a wealth of additional helpful sketches to illustrate the vehicles' versatile nature. Here the artist illustrates the ease with which heavy items can be loaded onto the Pick-up from the average loading bay, the vehicle's drop-down sides helping enormously in this task.

Essentially, Preis took Reuters's presentation of the Kombi as a dual-purpose vehicle and merely re-angled it to retain the original message of versatility, while also fully illustrating the rear hatch. In this instance, no doubt to avoid obscuring the view of the passenger-carrying Kombi, he opted to depict the rear hatch closed. While the delivery man wasn't far out of scale, the family travelling in the Kombi were smaller.

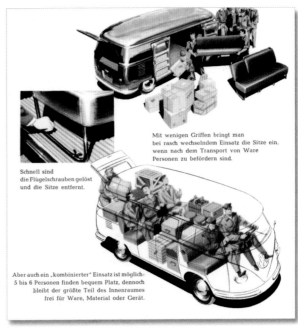

Mit wenigen Griffen bringt man bei rasch wechselndem Einsatz die Sitze ein, wenn nach dem Transport von Ware Personen zu befördern sind.

Schnell sind die Flügelschrauben gelöst und die Sitze entfernt.

Aber auch ein „kombinierter" Einsatz ist möglich: 5 bis 6 Personen finden bequem Platz, dennoch bleibt der größte Teil des Innenraumes frei für Ware, Material oder Gerät.

VW-Sieben- oder Achtsitzer

Rather than portray the Micro Bus with a full complement of passengers, Preis decided there was more impact if seven adults and a child were seen preparing to embark in what was now described as the "VW Sieben-oder Achtsitzser". In February 1956, Volkswagen had added a new option – a seven-seater alongside the established eight-seat model. The vehicle depicted was clearly an eight-seater (as evidenced by the full row of seats visible through the side doors).

Preis painted his Micro Bus in standard colours, and also did so with the Micro Bus De Luxe (below). The resulting glorious hues of Chestnut Brown over Sealing Wax Red lifted the image by at least one notch over the work of Reuters. He retained the pose created by his predecessor, and by opening the sunroof reinstated the cabriolet-like, luxury feel Reuters had created with his 1951 launch drawing.

VW-Sieben- oder Achtsitzer „Sonder-Modell"

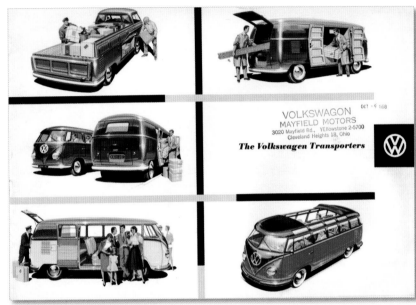

Preis's drawings were re-used in a number of generic brochures. The first of these (above) dates from 1957, and the second two followed the year after in large (right) and small format (below) respectively. The large brochures measured 298 x 210mm, while the handy smaller publications were a pocket-size 210 x 97mm.

Getting Ahead with Volkswagen Trucks

Kombi Station Wagon

Getting Ahead with the Volkswagen Transporter

For Preis the final years of the 1950s proved hectic in terms of reworks and new illustrations, at least as far as The Transporter was concerned. Updated general brochures demanded new drawings, both for covers and for interior pages in thumbnail and explanatory form.

His brief appears to have been to create either typical work or gentle lifestyle backgrounds for the covers, but more particularly to build an armoury of variations on established themes for internal pages. Preis re-coloured vehicles as paint options were updated, or added details as they became a part of the Transporter specification.

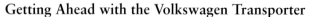

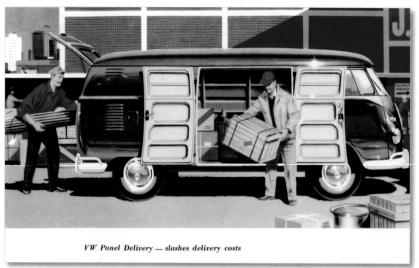

VW Panel Delivery — slashes delivery costs

The Larger Volkswagen for Large Families and Small Parties

Volkswagen Station Wagon and De Luxe Station Wagon

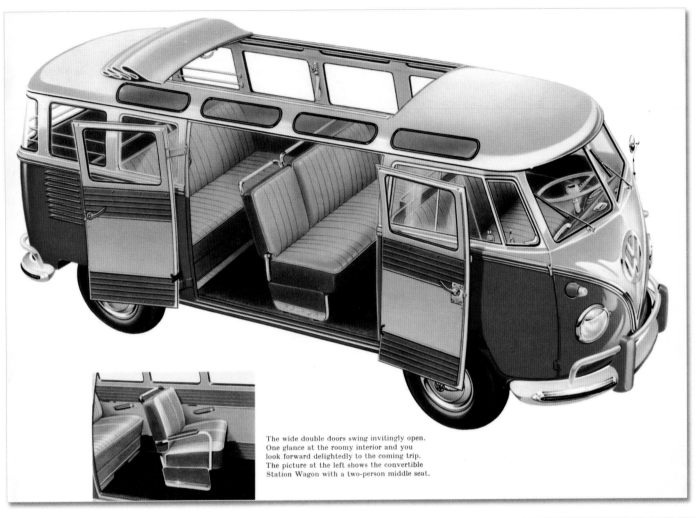

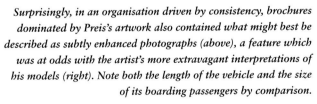

The wide double doors swing invitingly open. One glance at the roomy interior and you look forward delightedly to the coming trip. The picture at the left shows the convertible Station Wagon with a two-person middle seat.

Surprisingly, in an organisation driven by consistency, brochures dominated by Preis's artwork also contained what might best be described as subtly enhanced photographs (above), a feature which was at odds with the artist's more extravagant interpretations of his models (right). Note both the length of the vehicle and the size of its boarding passengers by comparison.

Although a double-cab Pick-up had been available as a special model for a few years, the task of promoting the vehicle only came to prominence after 3rd November 1958, when its manufacture was taken under the Hanover factory's wing. Charged with what could have been a rewarding task, Preis's attempt to handle its dual role – load carrying capacity with room for up to six in the cab – was far from ambitious, even if it was scrupulously accurate.

One relatively small (210x148mm) eight-page brochure of 1959 seemed sufficiently different to point a way ahead into the next decade. Its bright yellow cover appeared to indicate dynamic interior pages, but sadly the content and most of Preis's illustrations had been seen before.

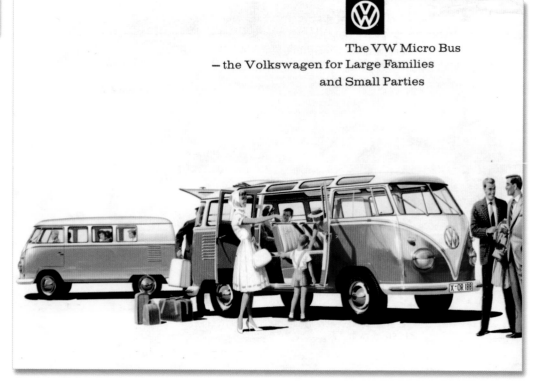

Instead of moving forward, Preis's final offerings, introduced in 1960 but lingering on into 1961, were essentially more of the same. The workaday Transporter version, which still carried its previous year's title, featured a plain-coloured background. On the other hand, his last passenger-carrying Transporter brochure carried a plain white background.

VW-KRANKENTRANSPORTER
UND -BEREITSCHAFTSWAGEN „WERKSMODELL"

The VW *Ambulance*

Call an Ambulance

The Ambulance evolved through four model specific brochures, from its birth in the final days of 1951 to the 1958 publication "VW Krankenwagen". In most ways, the Ambulance's story mirrors that of much faster-selling members of the range.

When the Ambulance was launched, Reuters turned it through 180 degrees so that its most important feature was emphasised. Volkswagen had reduced the size of the engine compartment and relocated the fuel tank to create a rear hatch through which a stretcher could be eased into the body of the Ambulance. Reuters chose to depict the Ambulance at night, which apart from increasing the dramatic atmosphere also allowed him to light the vehicle's interior, revealing its partially frosted windows and a glimpse of the safety bars protecting the window glass. The effect of a white Ambulance (in reality a relatively light beige shade) against a black background also highlighted such features as the roof-mounted ventilation fan. By showing the passenger side of the Ambulance, Reuters could also illustrate the side-loading doors and new lockable fuel filler flap.

Within a short time, allegedly in response to customer comments, Volkswagen revised the Ambulance so that the rear hatch was hinged at the bottom and supported by chains. Unusually, Reuters presented a completely new illustration of the vehicle (March 1952), rather than updating the original. Why he did this is far from clear, particularly as the setting was the same and the action of easing a stretcher and patient into the Ambulance was identical. There were improvements though: the rear of the Ambulance appeared slightly larger, the safety bars on the frosted windows were shown and even the fuel filler flap was more prominent, but none were sufficient to warrant a new drawing.

VW-Krankenwagen

Preis created his own version of Reuters's classic pose for the Transporter in 1956. He copied his predecessor's night-time scene but altered the angle, revealing the vast expanse roof panel. For once, Preis's exaggeration of the size of the vehicle in comparison to its driver and passenger was more pronounced than that of Reuters, while his stretcher was positively minuscule.

Come 1958, Preis prepared completely new artwork for the cover of a brochure with interior pages virtually identical to those of his 1956 offering. The artist cleverly placed his cream Ambulance against a concrete and glass building, thus helping the vehicle to stand out in what was a sunny daytime setting. While the act of easing a stretcher out of the Ambulance was still central to the story, the inclusion a second vehicle (complete with fully-finished headlamps and hinge-mounted spotlight) made the cover particularly eye-catching.

Preis also contributed one of his famous cutaway images depicting two Ambulances, one with two stretchers in use and the other with one folded away to create a second chair for a patient. This work was used in the 1956 brochure and after re-use in 1958, made its way into the next generation of special equipment brochures, which were released in 1961.

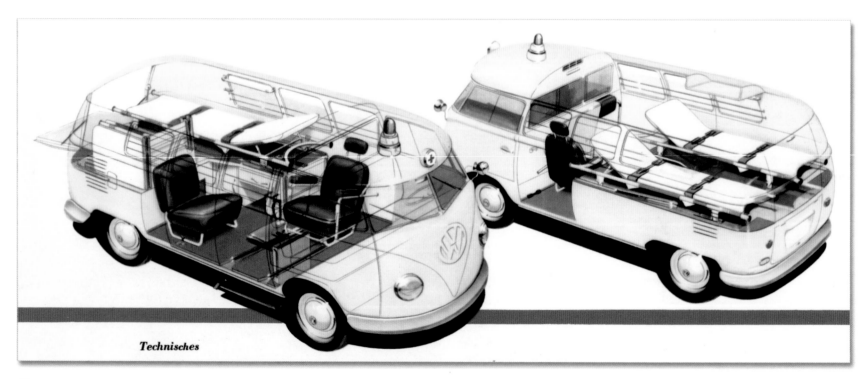

Getting into Ghia

The arrival of the Karmann Ghia coupé in the summer of 1955 posed a problem for Bernd Reuters. The car was longer and wider than the Beetle, whose platform and running gear it shared, and its curvaceous lines had an elegance the Beetle would always lack. For once, Reuters's device of exaggeration simply couldn't work. He tried it with disastrous consequences, but then, recognising the car for what it was, created a masterpiece that ranked alongside his finest.

The secret to the success of the image, first used as a cover in 1956, was Reuters's decision to portray a black Karmann Ghia at night. By doing so, the gleam of the chrome from the glow of the headlamps, the implied depth of gloss in the paintwork, and above all the aristocratic bearing of the lady driver seated in opulent surroundings, was all that was necessary to sell the car.

Reuters's accompanying internal three-quarter side profile of the Karmann Ghia, which employed his regular approach was, by contrast, very disappointing. From the bloated and frankly ugly nose cone, via slabby front and rear wings, to the unwarranted bulge of the roofline, the natural elegance of the Karmann Ghia was lost. Either Reuters or influential voices at Karmann or Volkswagen must have thought so too, for the following year this image had been replaced by a carefully retouched photograph of the car presented in the same pose.

Meanwhile, Reuters upgraded his already near-perfect cover image by changing the rich red but perhaps slightly garish upholstery to discreetly sumptuous black. Following the unwritten rule that red adds a focal point to any image, the artist changed the colour of his driver's dress from green to match.

Alongside Reuters's work, Karmann produced small-format brochures entirely reliant on photography to promote its wares. However, a second all-conquering cover was to emerge from the studio of the master in 1958.

Cover of the earliest version of one of Reuters' most attractive works, 1956.

During 1957 Reuters updated his Karmann Ghia at night image, removing the possibly garish red upholstery.

Probably Reuters's least attractive piece of work produced for Volkswagen. The artist's problem was that his normal tendency to elongate and exaggerate a vehicle only served to spoil what were the Karmann Ghia's near perfect lines. Both the wings and the nose cone of Reuters's car are particularly unattractive. 1956.

Unusually, Volkswagen sanctioned a purely photographic brochure to accompany Reuters's larger format offering. The format was small (210mm x 100mm) and extended to just four pages. The internal page imagery was restricted to a picture of the door and an edited photograph of the rear seat/luggage storage area.

With Reuters's unpalatable portrayal of the Karmann Ghia from a side perspective swept away, brochure compilers relied on carefully enhanced photography, while the use of tints of images of well-heeled owners offered a degree of sophistication befitting the car.

VOLKSWAGEN

KARMANN
Ghia

She's a Beauty

Although it might be assumed that Reuters would have opted to portray the new Cabriolet on the cover of the latest Karmann Ghia brochure when it was launched in August 1957, hard-headed sales potential probably demanded the artist offered a new interpretation of the Coupé, as both cars were presented in the ten-page brochure. Sadly, this deprived all of a Reuters interpretation of the Karmann Ghia convertible forever.

Reuters' new cover artwork not only successfully placed a white car, with a light coloured interior, on a white back-ground, but also accomplished what had previously been deemed unattainable previously. Reuters enlarged the Karmann Ghia's front wings and bonnet line and increased the curves of the frontal cone. In addition, he extended the car's length and splayed the visible rear wing from both the engine compart-ment lid and the main body of the car. The windscreen was more panoramic, the interior upholstery chunkier than reality and speed lines ran from one wheel to another.

Although Reuters's elected to place a man behind the wheel, the inclusion of the head of a pretty lady on the cover served the purpose of suggesting that a male owner could attract such a beauty by driving so sporty a Volkswagen.

The Volkswagen Karmann Ghia Cabriolet. Top up. Top down. Nobly styled. Mechanically delightful. For instance: the problem of how to open, push back and close the top quickly has been solved by a centrally-located handle. It can be turned easily with one hand while you remain seated. Half the top folds into the body. And, in spite of its soundproof padding, the top lies flat and blends in with the striking lines of the body.

Left and below: the internal page design of the latest Karmann Ghia brochure was entirely in keeping with the style of the car and far removed from the utilitarian approach adopted for the Beetle and the Transporter. Only the sophistication of the Beetle Cabriolet material came near.

KARMANN
Ghia

Imagine it is you seated there. Before your eyes this distinctive instrument panel. In your hands the streamlined wheel of this most remarkable car. The Volkswagen Karmann Ghia. There's nothing like her. She's the very essence of Beauty wedded to Common Sense. Ghia of Turin styled her ... masterfully. Karmann, noted custom body builder, transformed Ghia's genius of design into a shining reality ... superbly. One look. You like her ... enormously. Karmann Ghia is practicality. What else could make more sense than to power this marvel of design with the sturdiest, most dependable engine ever the same one that made the rugged, faithful air-cooled Volkswagen famous around the world. One drive. You want her ... tremendously. And why not? Nowhere else in the whole world of automobiles can you find such a happy combination of appearance, performance, riding comfort, and operating economy. Volkswagen's Karmann Ghia Coupé has a sister now - the Cabriolet - a very dream of a car bright, gay, and eager to let you learn again the real fun of driving blue skies, radiant sun, the wind in your hair, and a streamlined beauty that fairly hums with delight as she breezes along mile after mile.

VOLKSWAGEN

KARMANN
Ghia

Beyond the Grave

This later Karmann publication, a brochure that was still available at the beginning of 1962, was produced for the American market. From the start, Reuters had added a second tier to the car's bumpers for the US market. This was not a standard feature for European cars.

VW Karmann Ghia Coupé

With Volkswagen's new style of advertising already prevalent, Preis presented the Karmann Ghia Coupé and Cabriolet in a generic 1960 brochure devoted to all passenger-carrying Volkswagens.

The End of an Era

The brochure produced to promote the 1961 model year Beetle, when European models finally lost the semaphore indicators, remains something of an enigma.

Its cover apparently featured a new but unsigned work by Reuters, as well as several flat reinterpretations of his earlier more detailed illustrations on the inside. Almost by contrast, other pages carried virtually unaltered classic drawings by Reuters and Mundorff, the latter's work now beautifully reproduced in full colour. Appealing as this latest brochure was, the inclusion of the cover image of the Cabriolet brochure for 1960 tends to confirm that the designers worked hard to assemble something new out of existing material. It nearly worked but the result was more clinical and ultimately less successful.

Sadly, the formula that had once won Volkswagen accolades for its brochures was largely past its sell-by date. Something big was emerging out of America that would sweep the headlines and highlights of the 1950s away, and in so doing would generate countless more sales for Volkswagen.

Of the style of earlier years, but note how the car in the foreground has been turned to offer a frontal view.

THE 1960S

Such was the impact of advertisements created by American agency Doyle Dane Bernbach that, within a relatively short time from the firm's appointment in 1959, compilation brochures of its work were the norm.

Bill Bernbach and Ned Doyle were employed by the ultra-traditional Grey's agency before joining forces with Mac Dane to form DDB in 1949. Almost immediately they broke loose from what had become increasingly stilted convention.

In comparison to the promotional output of the US giants Ford, General Motors and Chrysler, Volkswagen's spend on advertising in America was minuscule, bordering on non-existent. The reason was simple. Growth in Beetle sales in America, from disastrously low numbers in the early 1950s to figures that forced Detroit to fight back with its own compact cars, had been achieved by word of mouth and VW dealers' hard work. In 1959, as rumours of homebred small cars started to filter through, Volkswagen dealers could offer nothing more than a six months wait for a new Beetle, and yet many people preferred this option to the conventional American gas guzzler.

The newly-appointed head of Volkswagen of America, Carl Hahn, had a two-fold concern on taking office. First, would mere reputation be sufficient to sustain annual sales in excess of 160,000 cars, and second, how should he react to stories of Detroit's determination to stem the aggressive tide of European imports, most notably the Beetle? Advertising appeared to offer the way forward.

In selecting DDB after three months of interviews and, according to Hahn, seeing in excess of 4000 advertising executives, his choice was radical. Conventional US advertising tended to make use of illustrations rather than photography, allowing exaggeration and enhancement to predominate. Similarly, airbrush work, sophisticated drivers, seductive females with hourglass figures, plus stately homes and town mansions, formed a background for the cars. The doctrine that had provided the foundations of US advertising was essentially one of dishonesty.

Bill Bernbach later told author Walter Henry Nelson that it was, above all, DDB's honesty that appealed to Hahn. "We didn't prepare anything special for them," said Bernbach of Volkswagen's delegation, "We just show prospects [potential customers] ads we've done for other clients. The only thing we try to sell them on is that we are advertising men and know our business. We told VW, 'You know your business better than we'll ever know it. But we know advertising better than you do'."

Bernbach then proceeded to recount how the agency immersed itself in Volkswagen's world. A whole team from DDB, including art director Helmut Krone and copywriter Julian Koenig, hurried to Wolfsburg. "We spent days talking to engineers, production men, executives, workers on the assembly line. We marched side by side with the molten metal that hardened into the engine, and kept going until every part was in its place. We watched finally as a man climbed behind the steering wheel, pumped the first life into the newborn bug and drove it off the line. We were immersed in the making of a Volkswagen and we knew what our theme had to be. We knew what distinguished this car. We knew what we had to tell the American public... We had seen the materials that were used. We had seen the almost incredible precautions taken to avoid mistakes. We had seen the costly system of inspection that turned back cars that would never have been turned down by the consumer. We had seen the impressive efficiency that resulted in such a low price for such a quality product. We had seen the pride of craftsmanship in the worker that made him exceed even the high standards set for him. Yes, this was an honest car. We had found our selling proposition."

An iconic headline contained on a two-sided brochure that grew out of a Doyle Dane Bernbach advert. While the text is different, the message is essentially the same (1960).

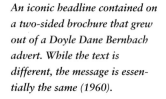

From this revelation emerged a campaign that, far from simply helping the Beetle to contend with Detroit's new small cars, produced consistent sales growth at a time when US imports from other European manufacturers plummeted. In 1962, when total imports had spiralled from the 1960 high of 614,131 cars to just 339,160, Volkswagen's rose to 200,000. DDB's philosophy of honesty was paramount in such success.

In such a vein, one advert declared that the Micro Bus had, "only a face a mother could love"; another declared (in the context of an engine set to last even longer than before), "The ... VW will stay ugly longer". DDB told the truth: the Beetle and Transporter were acquired tastes in terms of appearance.

Against a side profile of a Beetle occupying no more than 10 per cent of the page, the headline ran, "It makes your house look bigger", and in so doing offered the cleverest of confessions that the car was small. Similarly, a for once bloated headline, "If you wouldn't own a car in New York City, maybe you should buy a Volkswagen", confirmed that the Beetle was no lengthy limousine but an ideal vehicle to park on congested streets.

Where Detroit would claim an ambitious 30mpg for a new car that might achieve such a figure if driven with extreme caution, DDB presented the truth. Three Beetles were shown, each with a different miles-per-gallon figure. Nelson told the story of how a DDB employee reported that the point was to admit that there were people who got 24 miles per gallon, while others managed 32 and a small percentage even achieved 50mpg. The advert provided reality to its readers, rather than point scoring.

Where honesty wasn't foremost in the message, the words of Heinz Nordhoff were religiously adhered to. He'd declared the car must have an honest value: Volkswagens had to be perfect when they left Wolfsburg, the price had to be realistic, and they had to be built to last.

Complemented by a photograph of a seemingly perfect car, a one-word headline read, "Lemon". The car had been rejected by one of Volkswagen's 3389 inspectors because the chrome strip on the glove compartment was blemished!

Who but DDB could have presented a completely blank page where a photograph would normally reside? The headline announced that there was "No point showing the '62 Volkswagen. It still looks the same". Three neat, compact columns of text carefully announced a catalogue of subtle improvements, while not finding it necessary to state the obvious. The whims of stylists, and built-in obsolescence, were ignored at Volkswagen. Continual improvement of one model helped preserve resale values.

If the no-nonsense approach to imagery and eye-catching headlines worked, so too did the new approach to copy. DDB's copywriters addressed their audiences as intelligent readers, appreciative of honesty, the straightforward approach and humour.

Industry researchers quickly found that Volkswagen adverts were being read by many more people than average. Within a year of the start of the campaign, the work of DDB had become a talking point. Dealers found customers could recite the latest headlines with ease. Carl Hahn was delighted – so pleased that he dispensed with the services of Fuller, Smith and Ross, who had been asked to promote the Transporter 12 months earlier, and handed all Volkswagen's advertising to DDB, whose style enveloped all aspects of Volkswagen's many brochures over the next decade.

The famous "Lemon" advert.

Lemon.

This Volkswagen missed the boat.

The chrome strip on the glove compartment is blemished and must be replaced. Chances are you wouldn't have noticed it; Inspector Kurt Kroner did.

There are 3,389 men at our Wolfsburg factory with only one job: to inspect Volkswagens at each stage of production. (3000 Volkswagens are produced daily; there are more inspectors than cars.)

Every shock absorber is tested (spot checking won't do), every windshield is scanned. VWs have been rejected for surface scratches barely visible to the eye.

Final inspection is really something! VW inspectors run each car off the line onto the Funktionsprüfstand (car test stand), tote up 189 check points, gun ahead to the automatic brake stand, and say "no" to one VW out of fifty.

This preoccupation with detail means the VW lasts longer and requires less maintenance, by and large, than other cars. (It also means a used VW depreciates less than any other car.)

We pluck the lemons; you get the plums.

Our '63 truck has two (2) engines.

This year you can choose between two engines when you buy a VW Truck.

The one on the left is our standard model. (The legendary engine that made the VW famous!)

The one on the right is our new optional engine. It costs a little more, but then it's more powerful. (And it comes with bigger brakes!)

Say you generally carry a heavy load

Or say you have to do a lot of driving over steep, hilly terrain. Then, you'll probably want to take on our more powerful job.

Do you know some of the advantages in the VW power plant?

Both engines, for example, are air-cooled. So they can't boil over or freeze up.

Both are short-stroke, low rpm en-

gines. Which means less friction, longer engine life.

Both do about 24 miles to the gallon, take 5 pints (not quarts) of oil, and hardly ever need of between changes.

Both go in back of the VW. No matter which engine you choose, you're still getting the same old Volkswagen economy.

63 style.

More room. **More brrmmmmmm!**

This '63 Volkswagen is the most. It has more legroom in the cab and more power in the engine than any other VW Truck in 13 years.

There's more room to stretch your legs because the interior headlight mouldings have been flattened out. And a new adjustable driver's seat has been added. Just put the seat in reverse and slide it back until your legs feel comfortable. Then lock it in place.

Alongside is a new oversize passenger

seat, large enough for one well-upholstered rider. It's standard equipment.

Back in the engine room is our new air cooled 1500 (displacement is 1,500 cc, or 91.10 cu. in.) It's 25% larger and it develops 25% more horsepower than any other VW engine ever.

That's why this '63 truck can outsprint, outclimb, outdo any other VW Truck on the road today.

The engine – plus the larger brakes it

requires – is optional or extra cost. If you don't take it, you get our 1200 engine as standard equipment. That's the power plant that we've never stopped improving on.

Either way, you get an engine that averages 24 mpg, that can't freeze up or boil over, that's mounted in back for extra traction in snow, mud and sand.

What more could you want? Hmmmm?

Some Volkswagen owners look down on other Volkswagen owners.

When you graduate from a Volkswagen Sedan to a Volkswagen Station Wagon, you really step up in the world.

The Station Wagon stands a good foot taller than other cars.

And it holds more than the biggest conventional wagon you can find.

But the VW Wagon isn't only tall.

It's also short.

We saved 4 feet of hood in front by putting the engine in back.

Big as it is inside, it's only 9 inches longer than the Volkswagen Sedan.

So people who move up to the high-slung model still feel very much at home.

They park in the same little spots.

They still don't worry about freezing or boiling; the engine is air-cooled.

They still go a long way on a gallon of gas (about 24 miles) and a very long way on a set of tires (about 35,000 miles).

And it just tickles them to drive one Volkswagen and look down on a million others.

It's in the news—It's Advertised in . . .

TIME

THE WEEKLY NEWSMAGAZINE

THE VOLKSWAGEN KARMANN GHIA

The Volkswagen is the one in red.

These cars look alike to a Volkswagen mechanic.
They have the same engine, the same transmission, and the same chassis.
But the one on the bottom got mixed up with an Italian who thought our Volkswagen would make a sexy little runabout. Ghia of Turin.
The car's the VW Karmann Ghia.

Its special body takes so much hand work that we farm it out to one of Europe's greatest custom coachworks, Karmann of Osnabruck. Every seam is welded, ground down, filed and sanded by hand.
It's been mistaken for everything from a Ferrari to a Lancia.
Yet VW parts are all you need.
You get the VW's legendary mileage.

VW's air-cooled engine. And the famous Volkswagen traction in snow and sand.
Along with a gee-gaw or two. A defroster for the back window. Acoustical soundproofing. Adjustable bucket seats.
The price is quite a coup for a coupe like this. Hardtop, $2,295.* Convertible, $2,495.*
Hardly an arm and a leg.

The back cover of the Time *magazine advert brochure was devoted to one of DDB's cleverest Karmann Ghia stories.*

Dating from 1964, this is a page from an all-model advert brochure entitled, "How much longer can we hand you this line?", the line in question being the outline shape of the Beetle.

That's how many times we inspect a Volkswagen.

These are some of the ok's our little car has to get in our factory.
It's easy to tell the ok's from the no's. One no is all you ever see.)
We pay 5,857 men just to look for things to say no to.
And no is no.
A visitor from Brazil once asked us what

we were going to do about a roof that came through with a dent in it.
Dents are easy to hammer out.
So what we did shock him a little.
We smashed the body down to a metal lump and threw it out in the scrap pile.
We stop VWs for little things that you may never notice yourself.

The fit of the lining in the roof.
The finish in a doorjamb.
In the final inspection alone, our VW has to get through 342 points without one blackball.
One out of 50 doesn't make it.
But you should see the ones that get away.

For people who can't stand the sight of a Volkswagen.

Some people just can't see a VW.
Even though they admire its attributes, they picture themselves in something fancier.
We sell such a package.
It's called a Karmann Ghia.
The Karmann Ghia is what happened to a Volkswagen when an Italian designer got hold of it.

He didn't design it for mass production, so we wouldn't think of giving it the mass production treatment
We take time to hand-weld, hand-shape, and hand-smooth the body
Finally, after 185 men have had a hand in it, the Ghia's body is lowered onto one of those strictly functional chassis.

The kind that comes with VW's big 15-inch wheels, torsion bars, our 4-speed synchromesh transmission and that rather famous air-cooled engine.
So that along with its Roman nose and graceful curves, the Ghia has a beauty that is more than skin deep.

This DDB advert appeared in more than one small format brochure. The text refers to the car's beauty, the craftsman build and, of course, its "functional" Beetle chassis.

Amazingly even the American market Campmobile warranted a 12-page brochure devoted to its ads. With the title "Nature is grand. Also cold, damp, hard and buggy. Know what we did about it?", the adverts had featured, or were due to be run, in Field and Stream, Outdoor Life, *or* Sports Afield.

What's in it for the wife?

The VW Campmobile is for wives who'd rough it, if roughing it weren't so rough.
If your wife likes her great outdoors a touch more civilized, our Campmobile gives her the following touches (as standard equipment):
A double bed (for 2 adults). A hammock sleeps one child and a bench sleeps another.
An icebox with water tank and pump. A

dining table. 2 fold-away utility tables. Louvered screened windows. 2 reading lights. A clothing closet. A linen closet. 5 storage cabinets, and a 3-shelf pantry.
Fiber glass insulation keeps it cool when it's hot. And vice versa.
Your wife can't spend much time cleaning the walls (they're panelled in birch-grain plywood) or floor (it's carpeted with a textured vinyl compound) or uphol-

stery (that's vinyl too).
Options include a side-mounted tent that sleeps 2 more adults, and a ventilated roof section that pops up an extra 2 feet for increased headroom.
We put all these things in the Volkswagen Campmobile for her, just so we could get one thing in it for you.
Your wife.

This Volkswagen advertisement will appear in the May issues of Field and Stream, Outdoor Life, and Sports Afield.

Ugly **is only skin-deep.**

**Make sure you like it before you buy it.
You know how long Volkswagens last.**

The 1967 advert brochure entitled "The VW is Ugly Frivolous, Outrageous" encompassed all models. Beetle adverts were particularly self-denigrating, while at least one for the Transporter played on the vehicle's resemblance to a box. There was a need to reassure the American public that the latest addition to the range, known as the Fastback, was just as reliable and built to the same exacting standards.

Be sure to look for this familiar brand
on the front of every box.

*They didn't come much quirkier than
the 1969 advert brochure with the title
"The Typical Volkswagen Owner...".*

THE TYPICAL VOLKSWAGEN OWNER...

IS MARRIED... FORTY YEARS OLD...

UNDER THIRTY... SINGLE... HAS A Ph.D...

NEVER WENT TO COLLEGE... LIVES IN

THE CITY... LIVES IN THE SUBURBS...

CROSSED THE ATLANTIC
BY BOAT LAST SUMMER...

DOESN'T HAVE A PASSPORT... ALWAYS

TRAVELS BY AIR... OWNS HIS

OWN HOME... RENTS AN APARTMENT...

BOUGHT HIS VW IN THE PAST 12 MONTHS...

HAS OWNED HIS BUG 6 YEARS OR MORE

Why is a Volkswagen like no other car on the road?

Service is no problem to Volks-wagen owners. You will find excellent facilities at Authorized Volks-wagen Dealers in your own country and in 130 other countries throughout the world. A VW is serviced only by factory-trained technicians, schooled to demanding VW standards. Only Volkswagen-approved tools and equipment are used.

Costs are low. Service is fast. Authorized VW Dealers keep a comprehensive inventory of Genuine VW Spare Parts on hand. The Volkswagen is designed to last; and VW's preventive maintenance is planned to keep your VW ever young. Naturally you can expect the service you get to be as precise and efficient as the car itself.

Why is a Volkswagen like no other car on the road?

The impact of the first year of DDB's advertising campaign made its mark not just in America but also across Volkswagen's ever-expanding empire. It may have been assumed that when Carl Hahn spoke of the changing style and presentation of Volkswagen's literature he was restricting his comments to the USA, but this was far from the case. Instead, when the final series of Reuters's Beetle brochures debuted, they were almost as out-of-date in Europe as they were in Washington DC.

One of the first new-wave brochures made its way across the world between 1960 and 1961. The cover photograph depicted a frontal image of a black Beetle at night. While the car's bumpers varied according to the market (the US version, for example, depicted the two-tier arrangement favoured across the Atlantic, the home market version had single-tier) this was the only doctoring. Here was a straightforward cover, supported by equally honest photography throughout the publication's 22 pages.

Introductory text confirmed the Beetle to be, "An honest, functional car," with "timeless style," high resale value, and, above all, "designed to last, not to become obsolete." It was followed by merits of an air-cooled engine, four-wheel independent suspension, manoeuvrability, servicing (available in 130 countries throughout the world), build quality, space and comfort.

The brochure's biggest statement undoubtedly came from the photography – imagery far removed from what had been the norm in the 1950s. A combination of elegant simplicity and cleverly composed shots would be an ongoing theme of Volkswagen's output throughout the 1960s.

Volkswagen's roominess comes as an eye-opener to most people. All VWs actually have longer leg room in the front seat than many big cars—more head room, too. There is also space for a sur-prising amount of luggage. A generous luggage compartment is located under the hood. (The spare is here too, and you don't have to move anything to reach it.) Two large suitcases can be stowed in the carpeted, three-foot compartment behind the rear seat. The best-riding section of the car (the cradle between the four wheels) is reserved for the VW's passengers who travel in soft, form-fitting seats. The bucket seats in front adjust back and forth easily and independently, even while the car is moving. And the backs of the seats recline at three different angles for a change of pace on long trips, or a chance for a passenger to doze. The Volkswagen layout is essentially a functional one. Everything you need for handling the Volkswagen is conveniently placed within easy reach. This is the direct result of good planning. All the Volkswagen's instruments are in a practical cluster directly in front of the driver. The gear lever, the hand brake and the heater control fall to hand as naturally as your pocket. When you drive a Volkswagen, all you stretch are your legs. And you get all the niceties you expect a fine car to have: gas gauge, automatic windscreen washer, safety belt anchors, sun visors, coat hooks, assist straps, ashtrays—even a hand grip for the right front seat and a huge in-the-door pocket for the driver. Both doors are fitted with positive stay-open stops. Open the Volkswagen's extra-wide door and a bright overhead light goes on; you get an impression of trimness and serviceability. Drive it and you confirm the world-wide opinion: the Volkswagen is like no other car on the road.

Which is the shape of trucks to come?

In direct contrast to the universal nature of "Why is a Volkswagen like no other car on the road?" other new-style brochures were clearly directed at the US market alone. "Which is the shape of trucks to come?" (1960) is an obvious instance.

While the cover photograph was undoubtedly clever, most of the ten internal pages were in black-and-white, with a headline and three neat columns of text mimicking the layout of DDB's adverts. Most noticeable, though, was the similarity of copy style. The shortest of sentences, clever statements guaranteed to attract attention, and notably sentences that asked questions; each proved a hallmark of many a US-market brochure of the 1960s.

What generally might be termed 'question' brochures remained a theme of Volkswagen's advertising, regardless of model, throughout the 1960s, while other stories, or looks, proved far more transient. With the benefit of hindsight, it is

Cover and pages from "Which is the Shape of Trucks to Come?"

How does a one-ton truck chalk up against a Volkswagen?

We admit it. A standard one-ton truck carries 170 lbs. more than a VW.

But if you can squeeze by with 1,830 pounds of payload, look what a difference a Volkswagen can make.

Instead of a bulky giant, you'll be driving a nimble, sharp-cornering truck that knows how to keep out of traffic jams. An *empty* one-ton truck weighs more than a Volkswagen *fully* loaded. (About 4,200 pounds empty to VW's 4,079 pounds, fully loaded.)

You can operate two Volkswagen Trucks for what it costs you to operate a single standard one-ton truck.

You can park your Volkswagen in places that the average one-ton has to forego. A VW is three to five feet shorter. This means less time on the road, faster deliveries, more trips.

Tires, depreciation, insurance — they all cost you less.

If you never take a load under 2,000 pounds, no use talking. But if you do, talk to an authorized Volkswagen dealer right away. He'll show you operating cost figures.

Suggested retail price, East Coast Port of Entry.

Here's how much a Volkswagen Truck holds
a standard half-ton truck holds only the <u>white sets</u>

The VW is almost 3 feet shorter than a standard half-ton truck, yet it carries 830 pounds more.

Hard to believe, but true. Instead of half a ton, or 1,000 pounds, the VW Panel Delivery holds 1,830 pounds. Its cubic capacity is greater, too: 170 cu. ft. vs. 145 cu. ft. It costs only $1,895.*

The economic advantage is plain. For although the Volkswagen carries very much more, it costs only *half*

as much to run. Generally, you'll get about twice the gas mileage. And with about half the usual unladen weight there's only half the usual tire wear. The air-cooled VW engine needs no oil between changes and no anti-freeze at all. You also save on service, depreciation and, in many states, license fees and insurance.

You also save time. The Panel Delivery loads and unloads through big double side doors, as well as the rear door. Double doors on *both* sides are optional. So you not only load more into a VW; you load it faster.

Why not call your authorized VW dealer for a demonstration, operating cost figures and a cost comparison, today.

Suggested retail price, East Coast Port of Entry.

Why feed 'em when you don't need 'em?

Is it horse sense to pay the bill for horsepower you don't need?

A standard truck uses 90 to 175 horses to deliver normal light loads. Their gas and oil diet is loaded with calories. Only your wallet loses weight.

A Volkswagen Truck needs less horsepower because it has less dead weight to pull. The rugged, unitized steel body has no excess metal. The rear-mounted, air-cooled engine is all

muscle — no fat. There's no heavy drive shaft.

This is why the VW gas tank needs *half* the feeding that standard trucks demand. And the VW's nimble as a colt — gallops through the toughest traffic, turns corners sharper, parks in stalls standard trucks just don't fit.

A VW Truck can climb 25% grades fully loaded. And we mean loaded. A Volkswagen Panel Truck carries 1,830 pounds in 170 cubic feet of space. That's 830 pounds more than bigger, hungrier half-ton trucks.

Of course, your extra 'horses' are mechanical, but don't starve 'em. Trade them for a thrifty VW Truck. See your Volkswagen dealer soon.

Suggested retail price, East Coast Port of Entry.

relatively easy to answer the questions posed in the following brochure titles...

• "What's behind your Volkswagen?" 1961.
• "Why is the Volkswagen a favourite in 136 countries?" 1963.
• "Wie vielseitig ist der VW-Neunsitzer?" (How versatile is the VW Nine-seater?) 1963.
• "Do you like being alone?" 1964.
• "Wieviel werschiedene Volkswagen gibt es?" (How many types of VW are there?) 1965.
• "More choosy nowadays? Time you got a new car, then." 1966.
• "What sort of people drive VWs?" 1967.
• "Can you afford to drive another commercial?" 1967.
• "What do you expect of a new car?" 1968.
• "The VW Karmann Ghia. Is it really a sports car?" 1969.
• "Now can you see yourself in a Volkswagen?" 1969.
• "Why are some people prepared to pay more for the Karmann Ghia?" 1970.

Inevitably, the answer to the question posed on the cover of a 1962 Karmann Ghia brochure was, all people. Here's Volkswagen's full list: conventional people (Saloon), convertible people (open-top Karmann Ghia), city people (illustrated below), country people, travelling people (with cutaway image showing cases), stay-at-home people (cutaway showing children on the rear seat and groceries), thrifty people (car pictured with a petrol pump), spend-thrifty people (chauffeur and shopping), do-it-yourself people (man servicing his own car) and leave-it-to-Volkswagen people (VW mechanic servicing the car).

Several brochures carried the same question as a title. All outlined the Beetle's key selling points. This one, dated August 1963, was probably the cleverest in terms of its cover.

What kind of a car is a Volkswagen?

It's a new Volkswagen, the VW 1500 Sedan. A car that has more room than our VW. And more power. And more comfort.
But it's still a Volkswagen. With all of Volkswagen's famous engineering features and a few more besides.
The new, rugged 1.5 l engine (with 53 hp) is rear mounted and air cooled (of course). The gear box is fully synchronized (mais oui). The wheels are individually suspended by torsion bars (natürlich).
The VW 1500 accommodates up to five people (and their luggage) very comfortably.
In fact, there are two luggage compartments. one in the front under the bonnet, the other in back. (13.4 cubic feet altogether.)
Both are accessible from outside.
Where's the engine?
It's hidden under the rear luggage compartment. Its unique flat construction makes an additional luggage compartment possible.

The 1963 brochure "What Kind of a car is a Volkswagen?" was a relatively small-format, black-and-white publication measuring 160 x 210mm. The answer to the question posed on the cover was clearly intended to be all types of car. The pages reproduced here relate to the recently-launched VW 1500.

It's the Volkswagen 1500 Sedan with an all-sliding steel top.
Ideal ventilation for hot summer driving. Good for winter, too. (Just open it a few inches.)
Visibility in VW 1500 models is superb on all sides. The Sun-Roof Sedan even offers you visibility above. The front windscreen is high, wide, and curved. The rear window, too. Just take a look.
You can stretch out leisurely in any seat. The individual front seats (each 21.7 inches wide) are fully adjustable. You can lean way back, or sit up straight (seven positions), slide way forward or glide way back (seven positions).
Plenty of room in back, too — the rear seat is 51.1 inches wide.
Other built-in driving comforts include: ventilating system, heating system with demister, windscreen washer, windscreen wiper (speed adjustable), automatic locking of front seat backrests when doors are closed.

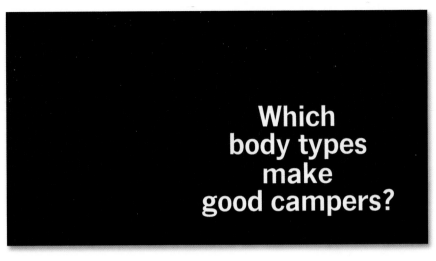

"Which body types make good campers?" was a North American exclusive, as VW of America sought to satisfy the demand for the Westfalia-converted VW Camper with locally built kits, or full conversions marketed as Campmobiles.

The answer to the question posed on the cover of the 1964 brochure "Want to buy a going business?" demanded an understanding of the dual nature of its interpretation. The proposition was that if you bought a, "Volkswagen Truck: It's a front office with a big backroom and power plant on wheels."

The headings to the images below were, "It's the Six-Passenger Pick-up for Ranchers, Gardeners, Farmers, Utilities, Contractors" and "It's the Station Bus for Road Shows, Hotels, Antique and Real Estate Dealers, Salesmen."

There was quite a contrast in styles between North American and European market brochures. "The VW Truck: is it too big for your business?" of 1965 was clearly American, answering its own question with a no. "Not if you have to deliver 792 one-lb loaves of bread... or 170cu.ft of flowers, or 325 pieces of dry cleaning," and, "not if you have to send out a crew to install a cable, or six guys to pick up some tomatoes."

The VW Truck: Is it too big for your business?

ECONOMY AUTOS LTD.
SOUTH FRANKLIN
MICHIGAN CITY, IND.
Ph. TR 2-9109

Dating from 1965, the 288 x 211mm, 16-page brochure "What's the VW Commercial got to write home about" was a typical example of the more conservative style of publication geared to Volkswagen's European market.

Moortown Motors Ltd,
Regent Street, Leeds, 2

What's the VW Commercial got to write home about?

Enjoy good company...
and good cars?

Here's something
that will interest you,
then.

The question posed on the suave and sophisticated cover of the brochure published in January 1967 to promote both models of Karmann Ghia, was in effect rhetorical. "Enjoy good company... and good cars?" appeared at the top of the cover in less than eye-catching print, to be followed by "Here's something that will interest you," further down the page. As the image of the Type 3 Karmann Ghia demonstrated, the overall message of the brochure was one of elegance in two cars that would never be commonplace on the road.

Like your car to be even faster?
Even more comfortable?
Even more exclusive?

Why do so many people buy Volkswagens?

"Why do so many people buy Volkswagens?" was an American-market special of 1968. The 18-page brochure consisted largely of full-page images of various owners and their Beetles. Eventually, on the last fold-out section, the cover question was answered with the headline, "Maybe it's word of mouth." The text epitomised the DDB style of brochure copy... "When most people have a good thing going, they want to share it with others. Friends tell friends. Neighbours tell neighbours. Even relatives who haven't spoken to each other for years start speaking again. And over the years, a lot of people must have listened to our story. Because our first year, we sold only two cars. But since then, we've sold over two million."

Two of the spreads from the first version of "Why do so many people buy Volkswagens?" At the time, the Beetle Antarctica 1 *was a famous car, while the inclusion of the Hollywood actor, Paul Newman's endorsement, speaks for itself.*

Why do so many people buy Volkswagens?

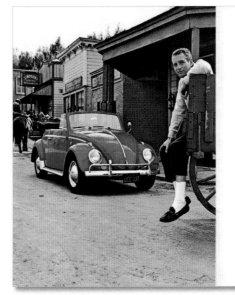

In 1969 a further version of "Why do so many people buy Volkswagens?" appeared carrying a percentage of identical photographs, but lacking headline quotes from owners. The cover, bearing a blue Beetle on a plain background, was a forerunner to what would become the norm in Europe in the 1970s.

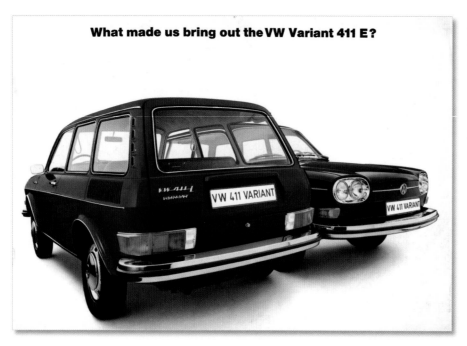

What made us bring out the VW Variant 411 E?

Following Nordhoff's death in April 1968, Volkswagen's air-cooled world started to fall apart. The 411, released at the end of the year, never really stood a chance. Deemed ugly by detractors from within, the brochure designer was wise to place emphasis on the rear-view of the estate version. Volkswagen's answer to the question posed on the cover was, "The tremendous success of the VW Variant 1600" and its, "genuine comfort, spaciousness and sure-footed chassis."

The Statement
A series of brochures lacking DDB's characteristic questions on their covers carried equally intriguing statements.

Making its debut in 1961, the eye-catching brochure "You can with a Volkswagen Micro Bus" at first glance appears to be intended for the North America market. However, this was not the case, as the alternative titles, "Sie können viel für sich tun – mit dem vielseitigen VW-Kleinbus" and "VW Car: possibilités illimitées" confirm. Compare the cover designed for the European market here with its USA contemporary below. The eagle-eyed will notice that even the vehicle specification (bumpers and indicators) vary.

You can
with a Volkswagen
Micro Bus

You can
with a Volkswagen
Station Wagon

For the US cover a troop of young baseball players replaced the European-market-friendly group of budding musicians seen above. Apart from confirming the rapid adoption of the DDB-style across the VW empire, note how the designer chose to overload both the American and European buses, risking a total of ten people in each instance.

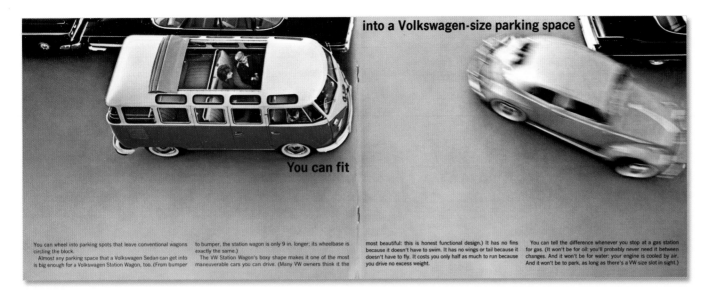

into a Volkswagen-size parking space

You can fit

You can wheel into parking spots that leave conventional wagons circling the block.

Almost any parking space that a Volkswagen Sedan can get into is big enough for a Volkswagen Station Wagon, too. (From bumper to bumper, the station wagon is only 9 in. longer; its wheelbase is exactly the same.)

The VW Station Wagon's boxy shape makes it one of the most maneuverable cars you can drive. (Many VW owners think it the most beautiful: this is honest functional design.) It has no fins because it doesn't have to swim. It has no wings or tail because it doesn't have to fly. It costs you only half as much to run because you drive no excess weight.

You can tell the difference whenever you stop at a gas station for gas. (It won't be for oil: you'll probably never need it between changes. And it won't be for water: your engine is cooled by air. And it won't be to park, as long as there's a VW size slot in sight.)

Just as the covers of "You can with a Volkswagen Micro Bus" varied according to which side of the Atlantic the brochure was intended for, so too did the headings for each double-spread and, if appropriate, the image. For example, for Europe, the line, "You can get service faster than for most domestic wagons," was replaced by, "You can get service in over 130 countries." The main double spread (above) was the same in both, despite the obvious presence of American limousines, but had been doctored to account for variations in bumpers and front indicators!

At roughly the same time as "What body types make campers?" was issued, Volkswagen of America released the eye-catching "Send this kit to camp". A six-page foldout brochure, measuring 330x183mm, its cover (right) intrigued the browser by illustrating all the components required to create a camper, but without any reference to the Volkswagen Transporter.

Opening the brochure revealed two further photographs. The first (below) depicted a VW Truck transformed to full camper mode and the second (below right), the same vehicle stripped of weekend pleasures and ready to act as a load carrier once more. This was clever marketing, as an acute shortage of genuine Campers coincided with plentiful supply of Delivery Vans.

Send this kit to camp

Incredibly simple but stunningly effective summarises this 1962 publication "Open for business", another American-market special. Made from the thin card needed to give a degree of rigidity, opening the fold-back "door" inset on the cover illustrated the vehicle's possible variety of uses.

With an air of predictability, the DDB title "Open for Business" had more significance than the words initially suggested. By opening the first small page, the front side of the second was revealed and the Station Wagon became a mobile office. Turned again, it developed into a vehicle carrying parcels and substantial topiary.

With the Beetle in centre position, the Station Wagon and Karmann Ghia to its left, and two models new to the US market on its right, this 1966 four-page range brochure intrigued due to its cover statement.

It took the skill of the copywriter to untangle the intentional conundrum of the statement. For the Beetle, he started by saying, "There are some things about our '66 Volkswagen people can't see. The 23 improvements. Mostly inside. Which is why our new VW looks the same as last year's model, even though we made it a better car."

Turning to the new models, both derivatives of the VW 1500 notchback, the copywriter overlooked the fact that the 'Squareback' (Variant) had been on sale in Germany and elsewhere for several years. Nevertheless, his statement was designed to guarantee the customer a no-risk purchase: "The Squareback Sedan may look new but it has nine million Volkswagens of experience behind it."

Cleverest of all, though, was the copy for the genuinely new Fastback: "Is the Fastback a new kind of car? Or is it the familiar Volkswagen? Yes... So, if anyone should ask, you can tell him that outside the Fastback is a new kind of car. Inside it's all Volkswagen."

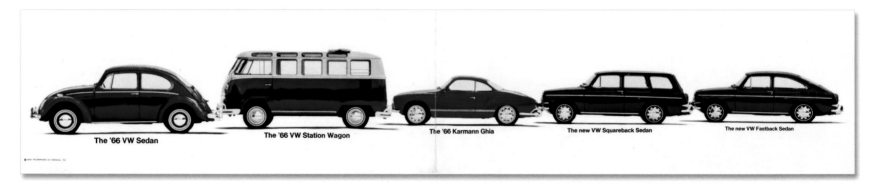

Next time you go for a drive in the country

With the sun dipping in the evening sky, or just making its appearance at the start of a new day, the getaway freedom of this 1967 cover image prompted a longing to purchase a Campmobile.

While two of the brochure's eight pages were devoted to the Campmobile's versatility as a practical vehicle for weekday use, the main thrust of the publication was in the direction of Volkswagen's ability to offer leisure and relaxation.

Pages two and three brought to mind the same feelings as those on the cover: "Spend the weekend in your Volkswagen house-in-the-country. There's room. This Volkswagen has space for a family of four to eat and sleep. Because it's a Campmobile.

"On the road, the Campmobile gets about 23 miles to a gallon of regular gas. The rear-mounted engine gets you through sand, snow and mud. And the air-cooled engine never freezes or boils. Because it's a Volkswagen.

"Back in the city, this Volkswagen still has more room for people than you'll probably ever need. And for more groceries than you'll eat in a month. Because it's a Station Wagon.

"We're not saying the Volkswagen Campmobile is three vehicles in one. But we're not saying it isn't."

don't come back until Monday morning.

Spend the weekend in your Volkswagen house-in-the-country.
There's room.
This Volkswagen has space for a family of 4 to eat and sleep. Because it's a Campmobile.
On the road, the Campmobile gets about 23 miles to a gallon of regular gas. The rear-mounted engine gets you through sand, snow, and mud. And the air-cooled engine never freezes or boils. Because it's a Volkswagen.
Back in the city, this Volkswagen still has more room for people than you'll probably ever need. And, for more groceries than you'll eat in a month. Because it's a station wagon.
We're not saying the Volkswagen Campmobile is three vehicles in one.
But we're not saying it isn't.

Das ist nicht das, was Sie denken.

The arrival of a new Transporter in summer 1967 was big news for Volkswagen. It represented the first time an existing model hadn't simply been improved in the manufacturer's 22-year post-war existence. While brochure output inevitably rocketed and a plethora of themes emerged to tell the new Transporter's story, the two included here tend to illustrate the difference between DDB-led activities in the USA and what was specifically designed for European use.

Of the two cover headlines, probably "Das ist nicht das, was Sie denken" (left) was more intriguing, while the brashness of the cover image of the US Station Wagon brochure (below left) provoked greater temptation to peep into the pages. Both brochures were map-style foldout affairs, each forming the equivalent of eight pages.

At first, the German brochure appeared more conservative, with formal layout and pictures arranged symmetrically. In reality, though, it was an extraordinary way to proclaim existence of a new model.

The German tale was the story of the Kombi, which with its panoramic windscreen and new dashboard (hence the cover statement), might easily be mistaken for a passenger car. Each headline confirmed the supposition: "That's not what you think. It's a workplace. But with all the comforts of a saloon. The new VW transporter provides driver comfort (more than many a saloon)... while also providing a convenient loading space."

By contrast, the less formal layout of the American design, and rather disappointing repetition of what was probably a pre-production press image, detracted from the overall effect. However, the US brochure's writer made up the lost ground: "The most noticeable change is that you can notice the change... From the driver's seat you can see more of what's ahead... There are also many changes that you won't be able to see. You'll feel them when you drive the '68."

Es ist ein Arbeitsplatz.

Ein Arbeitsplatz im neuen VW-Transporter. Ein Arbeitsplatz, auf dem Sie es sich bequem machen können. Und auf dem Sie eine gute Übersicht haben.

Weil er eine größere, gewölbte Windschutzscheibe hat, die hoch ins Dach gezogen ist. So hoch, daß Sie auch hohe Ampeln ohne Verrenkungen sehen können.

This year, as usual, we've changed the Volkswagen Station Wagon.

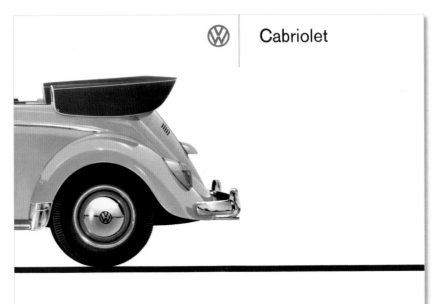

Cabriolet

Der Wagen mit eigener Note

Es sind gewiß nicht die schlechtesten Kenner des Automobils, denen es auf sportliches Fahren im offenen Wagen, in Luft und Sonne ankommt, die neben technischen Ansprüchen auch auf den Komfort besonderen Wert legen und ein Auto mit eigener Note erstreben. Für solche Feinschmecker haben Konstrukteure und Karosseriebauer kompromißlos ein Voll-Cabriolet geschaf-

fen, zeitlos schön in Linie und Form, mit völlig versenkbaren Seitenteilen - einen Wagen für verwöhnte Automobilisten, doch ohne überhöhte Ansprüche an die Brieftasche. Er zeichnet sich aus durch hervorragende Fahreigenschaften, ist hoch in der Leistung, aber niedrig im Anschaffungspreis und sparsam im Unterhalt. Sein nobler Stil wird durch die harmonisch aufeinander ab-

When half a car was better than a whole one

The notion of producing a cover and, in some cases, internal pages that only included part-images of the vehicle, was relatively short-lived.

The Beetle is best represented in this instance by the Cabriolet, mainly because the half-car theme extended to more than one edition and, as a result, survived longer than most. Measuring 295x210mm, as did all the other brochures in the initial series, the 1961 Cabriolet story extended to six pages, after initially folding out to four. Although the front cover carried nothing more of the vehicle (above) than part of its rear quarter, the back cover depicted the remainder of the car. With both covers splayed out, the Cabriolet became a complete car.

Inside, the car's dashboard, pedal arrangement and front seats formed one image. The rest of the car was cropped by a bold black line, which ran across the adjacent pages, this time depicting the car with hood down, cut off about half-way down the driver's door by the dominant black line. The final image was a complete hood-up Cabriolet resting its wheels on the now-famous black line.

With sufficient text, clear headings and a plain white background, the effect was strikingly avant-garde. Many decades after it was designed, the style hasn't dated – even though, in the eyes of the avid brochure collector, it lacks the appeal of work by Reuters.

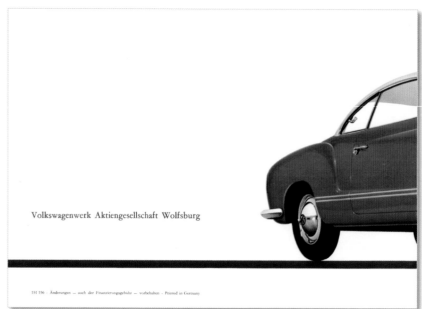

Volkswagenwerk Aktiengesellschaft Wolfsburg

The new-style Karmann Ghia brochure of 1961 was remarkably similar, albeit including more pages to show several models. Similarities included the dominant black line, portrayal of one of the car's distinctive features – the carefully sculpted and nose – on the front cover, which combined with the rest of the car on the back cover to produce a full-length image, and a fold-out sheet. The page tally had increased to ten, with both Coupé and Cabriolet shown in profile on separate two-page spreads. Although a dashboard cleverly sat on the black line, and the steering wheel not only extended over the line but also fell off the page, other images unfortunately carried a hangover from previous years.

Interieur

Dem strahlenden äußeren Gesicht des Karmann-Ghia entspricht das geschmackvoll gediegene Interieur. An der übersichtlich aufgegliederten Armaturentafel befindet sich in sinnvoller Anordnung alles, was man zur zuverlässigen Kontrolle und sicheren Fahrt benötigt. Unmittelbar vor dem sehr griffigen, angenehm in der Hand liegenden Zweispeichen-Lenkrad (mit Hupring, Blinkerschalter und Lichthupe) sitzt das Zentralinstrument mit Tachometer, Kilometerzähler und sämtlichen Kontroll-Leuchten, darüber der Kraftstoff-Anzeiger, rechts neben diesem die Zeituhr. Vom Fahrersitz aus werden auch die fein regulierbare Frischluftanlage und der Verschluß der vorderen Haube bedient, der beim Cabriolet noch gesondert abschließbar ist. Die kräftigen, weit ausholenden Scheibenwischer und die serienmäßige Scheibenwaschanlage gehorchen von einem kombinierten Zug-Dreh-Schalter aus. In der Mitte der Armaturentafel ist für den Einbau des Radiogerätes vorgesorgt; rechts, neben dem Kipp-Ascher, befindet sich ein sehr geräumiger, breiter Handschuhkasten mit Schnappschloß. Der Luftklappenzug entfällt dank der Startautomatik des Vergasers. Der Sicherheit des Beifahrers dient ein elastischer Haltegriff; die obere Wölbung der Instrumententafel trägt in ihrer ganzen Breite einen Kunststoff-Blendschutz.

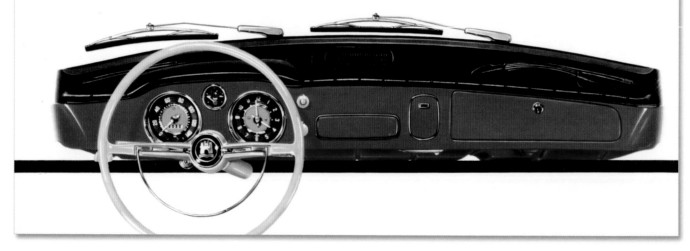

VW 1500

New for 1961 was the VW 1500. Inevitably, promotional material had been prepared in abundance in advance of the launch and, while not entirely uniform in style, the core range of brochures featured no more than part of the car on the cover.

The six-page 295x210mm brochure designed to promote the new VW 1500 saloon, or notchback, depicted the car at just about every conceivable angle, emphasizing its modern and relatively luxurious interior and, thanks to the flat suitcase design of its 1493cc upgrade of the Beetle engine, its capacious carrying capacity. However, it was only through reading the brochure text that it became obvious where the engine was – under the rear boot!

The inclusion of a side-view of the Beetle reinforced the message that although the saloon was a new car, a vehicle radically different in its appearance to Volkswagen's original model, it was also built on all the tried and trusted characteristics of a vehicle now approaching the 5,000,000 production mark.

Curiously, cover wording on the brochure, a simple "VW 1500", made no play of the fact that the car was new – unlike print produced to promote the soft-top version.

New, thoroughly tested

The VW 1500

A Volkswagen product

Everybody knows the Volkswagen. Now, the new, larger VW 1500 is being introduced. The Volkswagen factory has no intention of replacing the renowned and successful Volkswagen. The VW 1500 is an addition to the production range, resulting from an ever-increasing public demand for such a product. All the know-how of Europe's largest automobile factory, with nearly five million vehicles on the world's continents, has gone into its manufacture. • The air-cooled engine, which is in a higher performance class (SAE 53 bhp at 4000 rpm), is situated under the easily accessible, insulated luggage compartment in the rear. Its new flat construction gives the car a second luggage compartment. Utility rather than novelty has been the guiding principle of the design, as shown by the neat, well-balanced lines. The practical body offers a roomy, comfortable interior, and its low centre of gravity is one of the reasons for the car's excellent roadholding. Streamlined, pleasing to the eye, its honest styling will be as valid tomorrow as it is today. Rear visibility is especially good, with sturdy pillars between the windows ensuring maximum rigidity. The large-sized wheels and brake surface create a margin of brake safety unique in this class of automobile. Special, newly designed low section tyres result in greater side stability, hence unusually good cornering qualities. The oil cooler guarantees operating safety at all temperatures, and at sustained high speeds. The VW 1500 is a practical car for drivers wanting the utmost in value and economy. The superior design, highest quality in materials, workmanship and finish, a close network of VW service facilities and workshops, all contribute to the lasting excellence of this exceptionally well-planned car.

Presenting the new VW 1500 Convertible

If proof positive was required that brochures were prepared in advance of a model, the 1961 VW 1500 Convertible is a prime example. Despite a headline on page four proclaiming the Convertible to be, "Elegant and sophisticated, tough and rugged," the car didn't go into production because Karmann, who was responsible for the soft-top model, couldn't provide sufficient body rigidity!

Page two of the VW 1500 Convertible brochure (right) sat alongside page four (bottom, right) to produce a full image of the car with its hood up. It was only when the six page publication was fully opened up that page two matched with page three (bottom, left), revealing the Convertible in all its glory with the hood down.

A sporty, elegant car, bound to be among the elite in its class. Style and luxury are combined with the economy, ruggedness, and reliability of the VW 1500 Sedan. On sunny days, the top folds down quickly and smoothly, covered by a boot matching the colour of the car. With side windows fully lowered, the matchless body styling offers the utmost in driving pleasure. Or with the hood up, a well-padded, completely sealed protection against wind and weather. The curved windscreen, made of safety glass, is a unique feature for convertibles. Rear visibility is also exceptionally good. The VW 1500 seats four or five persons comfortably. The two luggage compartments, front and rear, offer ample room for luggage or camping equipment. Though easily accessible from without, both are secured from within as a precaution against theft. The flat constructed, insulated engine is mounted under the rear luggage compartment, creating maximum space for occupants and luggage, at the same time conserving the car's practical dimensions, so essential in modern traffic.

VW 1500 Station Car

Slightly after emergence of the 1500 brochures, Volkswagen added a further duo. One was specifically designed to promote what for the British market was mistakenly called by the Americanism of the "VW 1500 Station Car"; the other embraced the full family of models. The reason for a later publication date in both instances was that the variant (estate) didn't start to roll off the assembly line until the early months of 1962.

That brief period nevertheless saw a slight realignment in VW 1500 cover styles, so that while the clever subtlety of the whole car being absent remained the central theme, no longer were the vehicles' lower panels unceremoniously cropped off on the designer's board. In making this change, they strengthened the association between the VW 1500 and the likes of both the Beetle Cabriolet and the Karmann Ghia.

Smart-looking sedan

and handy commercial in one

Attractive, practical, and robust

Do you want a fast, elegant passenger car? Here you have it. Do you want a light, roomy, and thrifty commercial vehicle? Here it is. Both wishes are fulfilled in the VW Station Car. By its many and varied uses, the new VW 1500 Station Car bridges the gap between a comfortable sedan and the VW Kombi, an essentially larger commercial. Besides, it is a genuine VW, constant in performance and economy, a practical car through and through.

Take a look at the VW 1500 Station Car, inside and out. Try the side doors, the rear door, the hood. Sit behind the steering wheel. Note the ample passenger room, the loading surface and capacity. Apply the most exacting standards, and you will come to the objective conclusion: an astounding car. It is an attractive, comfortable car of the medium class, affording unusual space for luggage or what have you. It is just as suitable for use as a service car for well-known firms, as it is for independent business and trades, in fact, in all situations where a VW Commercial is too large and the usual standard passenger car is too small.

The modern, streamlined body, whose roof extends its full height to the rear of the car, makes the combining of a Kombi and a Sedan in the VW 1500 Station Car possible. The body design creates a larger load capacity, without losing the character of a passenger car. This maximum of usable room is primarily due to the position and design of the engine, which is flat in construction and mounted low. Such an arrangement permits the level, rubber-covered floor, and hence, the advantageous loading height.

The rear door is almost as wide as the car. It can be opened completely and fixed at the extended position, and is lockable from outside. Under the front hood, however, in the space usually occupied by the engine in most vehicles, the VW 1500 Station Car offers an additional roomy luggage compartment – absolutely unique in this class of car.

The front seats and the upholstered rear seat offer comfortable seating for four or five persons. The loading space to the rear can be extended more than half by folding the rear seat backrest to the front.

The VW 1500 Station Car as a Kombi-Sedan, is an ideal car for professional and business men, for leisure time and weekends. With its unusually large luggage space, it is also the ideal holiday car on long journeys for motorists and their entire families. Luggage trailers, roof-racks — all such items, requiring additional expense and bother, are unnecessary with this car.

All about the VW 1500 Range –
a New Line of Volkswagens

Volkswagenwerk AG · Wolfsburg · Germany

151 202 18 · Specifications subject to change without notice · Printed in Germany

The VW 1500 range front cover story was clearly presented as linking the new 1500 to the legendary Beetle. Indeed, more of the original Volkswagen was on view! And it was only when the front cover (top, left) was placed flat with the back one (top, right) that the whole of the the VW 1500 was revealed. Despite the logical extension to 20 pages, the 1962 vintage brochure still measured 295x210mm, but the overall attraction was the first appearance of manicured models. Suddenly, carefully staged imagery benefited from the added dimension of equally meticulously posed people who could turn a hint into a full-blown tale. For example, the inclusion of a boy and his mother manoeuvring an inflatable fish into the Convertible immediately conjured up the pleasurable lifestyle vision of a weekend by a lakeshore or at the sea – an agreeable experience more readily accessible through ownership of a VW 1500 Convertible.

What has it got to offer?

Plenty of space, a beautifully finished two-tone interior, and many practical features to make driving pleasant and enjoyable.
The VW 1500 is 166.3 inches long, bumper to bumper, offering a very comfortable and spacious interior. This car is easy to manoeuvre. Easy to handle. Easy to park. And fun to drive.
Once you open the very wide doors (42.1 inches), they stay open by themselves. Once you close them, they stay closed. No rattles. Both doors can be locked from the outside as well as the inside.

You have easy access to all seats. The two deeply cushioned bucket-type front seats can be individually adjusted for maximum comfort. Forwards for short legs. Backwards for long legs. The back-rest at different angles (all in all: 49 different positions are possible.) The front seats are very wide, 21.7 inches each.
When the doors are closed, the seat backs are automatically locked into position so that they can't tilt forward should you have to apply the brakes suddenly.
And the rear seat? 53.1 inches wide. With arm-rests on either side and one in the middle which can be folded back. Very comfortable.

Why is this convertible like a sedan?

Everybody knows that it is fun to drive a convertible with its top down. Plenty of fresh air. And plenty of sun.
But what if the sun doesn't shine? What if it rains? Or snows? Or is just nasty outside?
That is when this VW 1500 Convertible has a very definite advantage. Its top. (It is more than just a piece of waterproof cloth.) When you are inside the car, you don't see any ugly struts or crossbars. Only a smooth and beautiful canopy. The entire roof protects you from cold and noise.
And how quickly it is opened or shut. And how closely it fits. No water gets into this convertible. Even when you spray it with your gardenhose full on. In case you want to wash it for instance. Please look at the rear window. It's big – like in a sedan. And it

is not just plastic – it's real glass. It is safety glass. As are all the windows on every Volkswagen.
When the top is folded down, you can hardly see it. That is what gives this automobile its clean, simple, elegant look.
That is how a convertible should be made.
For open-air driving? By all means.
But you should also have a roof over your head. And it should be nice and cosy inside.

96

VW 1500 Karmann-Ghia-Cabriolet

Nun, zu diesem Verdeck ist einiges mehr zu sagen als nur, daß es sich leicht öffnen und schließen läßt: das Auffallendste ist wohl die große flexible Rückscheibe, die dem nach rückwärts sichernden Blick genügend Raum gibt, um die Fahrbahn in voller Breite zu sehen. Dem Verdeck wird durch die dicke Wattierung, die den Bezug formt, seine weiche und strömungsgünstige Rundung gegeben. Zudem isoliert die Wattierung gegen Kälte wie ein Stahldach. Im Cabriolet sitzt man an eisigen Tagen ebenso wohlig warm wie in einer Limousine. Überdies aber schluckt das Verdeck in stärkstem Maße alle Geräusche; im VW 1500 Ghia-Cabriolet fährt man besonders ruhig.

Ein starkes Scherengitter trägt das Verdeck und verbindet es an der Frontscheibe über einen kräftigen Querholm mit dem übrigen Wagenkörper zu einer festen Einheit.

Das VW 1500 Karmann-Ghia-Cabriolet ist mehr als irgend ein Auto, es ist gewiß die vollkommene Erfüllung eines automobilistischen Wunschtraumes. Aber – wir möchten sehr realistisch dazu sagen: zu mäßigen Gebühren. Ist es überhaupt noch notwendig, daß wir Sie zu einer Probefahrt bitten? – Sie sind uns jederzeit herzlich willkommen.

Volkswagenwerk AG · Wolfsburg

Überreicht durch: SCHMIDT & HOFFMANN
KIEL
Lerchenstraße 15 · Königsweg 76-78
Andreas-Gayk-Str. 19-21 · Karlstal 25
Telefon 4 4791

151 324 / Änderungen vorbehalten · Printed in Germany

There was one further derivative of the VW 1500. This was the Karmann Ghia, a car originally proposed as both a Coupé and Cabriolet. Unfortunately, the latter didn't see series production. However, as with the VW 1500 Convertible, a brochure was produced in 1961 before the decision was made to terminate the project.

Extending to no more than four pages and smaller in size (265x202mm), it had the Cabriolet on the front cover from windscreen backwards (above left), and on the back cover from front boot lid forwards (above right). The car's radical razor-edge frontal styling wasn't prominent.

VW 1500
KARMANN
Ghia

Destined to be the slowest seller in Volkswagen's range in the 1960s, and a model Nordhoff was looking to replace at the time of his death, the VW 1500 Karmann Ghia Coupé represented the most drastic departure from anything so far approved for production. With styling characteristics that make it more pleasing to the eye nowadays than in the 1960s, and geared to the fashions of the American market rather than the natural conservatism of Europe, perhaps inevitably the first VW 1500 Karmann Ghia Coupé brochure, produced in 1961, and a 269x205mm, 16-page publication, was as avant-garde as the vehicle it was designed to promote.

The front cover took the half-car style to extremes, portraying no more than a glimpse of the steering wheel, part of the windscreen, the driver's-side window, a fragment of the roof lining and virtually indistinguishable black exterior panels. However, as a young and obviously affluent couple were peering through the window with a mixture of admiration and desire in their eyes, the cover worked, as did the equally modern internal pages.

Internal spreads. Even the use of a car painted black, added to the feelings of built-in extravagance.

Back up a little. To get the whole picture.
Three things make a car a Karmann Ghia:
● Design by Ghia of Turin.
● Body by the Karmann coachmakers of Osnabruck.
● Engine and gear box and chassis by Volkswagen of Wolfsburg.
The VW Karmann Ghia 1500 is the second Karmann Ghia. (It doesn't take the place of the one before; we still make the original Karmann Ghia.)
It gives you more room than the first. More comfort. More power.
Because it's a limited-production car, it's built like a custom car. And it looks it.
Example: Fenders are hand-welded in continuous seams, not spot-welded. They're hand-sanded, your hand can't find these seams; steel flows into steel without a trace.

Come inside. And look around you. Settle down in either of the deep bucket seats. They're softly upholstered. Contoured. 23 inches wide.
They adjust to you. Slide backward and forward. Change pitch to let you stretch out or sit up high and look around.
Look at the dashboard. Its recessed instruments. Its clock. Its padded ledge. (Sunlight won't bounce back in your eyes.)
Notice the niceties. Big pockets in the doors. Long arm rests. Recessed handles.
Looking for the heater? It's built into the car. Along with the defroster. (There's even a defroster for the rear window.)
And the fresh air ventilator.
Push button for the windscreen wipers. Notice the blades. They're curved - to fit the glass.
And try the windscreen washers. Just push the next button to start the spray. (Its force: compressed air from any tyre pump.)

Take a turn. See how it corners.
There's no swing. No sway.
No feeling you're losing control.
There's no jolting. Little, if any, road noise. Or engine noise.
Or vibration.
Not around sharp curves. Or over deep ruts. Or down sudden dips in the road.
The reason: All four wheels have independent springing, independent torsion bars. Moreover, a stabilizer counteracts roll tendencies.
Here you see the front torsion bars. A new design.
Because they're crossed in an "X", and not held in the middle, they're longer and springier.
Result: a softer, more comfortable ride.
Other reasons for your comfort and stability:
Rubber mounts on axle, frame and subframe.
Large rubber stops to keep the wheels from bottoming. And wide balloon tires.
More rubber on the road.

To coincide with the upgrade in 1963 from single to twin carbu-rettors for the VW 1500 Karmann Ghia (and other models in the range), what appeared to be the same brochure was re-issued and the text duly amended. However, apart from cropping the cover image to depict even less of the car and deleting all reference to the model, the general approach was also softer and more casual. This subtle change is evident in the removal of the male model's starchy hat and through the amended pose of the lady in the bottom spread reproduced on this page.

Come inside.
And look around you.

Settle down in either of the deep
bucket seats. They're softly
upholstered. Contoured. 23 inches wide.
They adjust to you. Slide backward and
forward. Change pitch to let you stretch out
or sit up high and look around.
Look at the dashboard. Its recessed
instruments. Its clock. Its padded ledge.
(Sunlight won't bounce back in your eyes.)
Notice the niceties. Big pockets in
the doors. Long arm rests. Recessed handles.
Looking for the heater? It's built
into the car. Along with the defroster.
(There's even a defroster for the rear window.)
And the fresh air ventilator.
Push the button for the windscreen wipers.
Notice the blades. They're curved
to fit the glass.
And try the windscreen washer.
Just push the next button to start the spray.
(Its force: compressed air from
any tyre pump.)

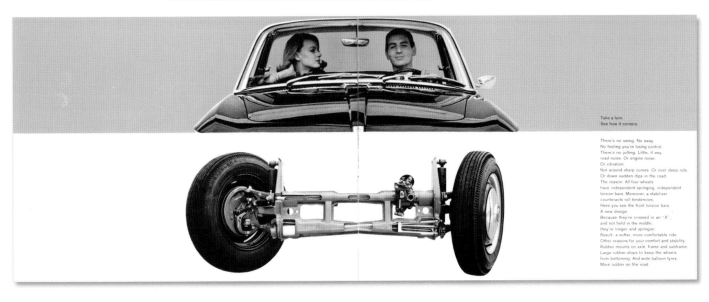

Take a turn.
See how it corners.

There's no swing. No sway.
No feeling you're losing control.
There's no jolting. Little, if any,
road noise. Or engine noise.
Or vibration.
Not around sharp curves. Or over deep ruts.
Or down sudden dips in the road.
The reason: All four wheels
have independent springing, independent
torsion bars. Moreover, a stabilizer
counteracts roll tendencies.
Here you see the front torsion bars.
A new design.
Because they're crossed in an "X",
and not hold in the middle.
they're longer and springier.
Result: a softer, more comfortable ride.
Other reasons for your comfort and stability.
Rubber mounts on axle, frame and subframe.
Large rubber stops to keep the wheels
from bottoming. And wide balloon tyres.
More rubber on the road.

Open the door

A near contemporary of the second edition of the VW 1500 Karmann Ghia brochure was the new Beetle-based Karmann Ghia publication, which again featured a cover with only a fragment of the car showing. This was "Open the door", a 16-page (including fold-outs) largely-pictorial brochure, measuring a compact 232x210mm and giving a virtual tour through the door of the car.

The unusual three-page foldout image (below) was designed to illustrate the Karmann Ghia's luggage carrying capacity (centre and right) and the owner's ability to change from luggage space to additional seating through the expedient of a tip-back bench seat (left). In their quirky way, the designers thought it unnecessary to include a further front section of the car, despite the eye's natural tendency to scan the page from left to right.

But it's practical, too

THE VOLKSWAGEN CAMPER

WITH WESTFALIA DE LUXE EQUIPMENT

As VW Camper sales began to escalate towards the end of the 1950s, particularly so in the USA, Volkswagen decided to produce brochures to market the latest conversions by the German firm Westfalia. Generous in size at 296x210mm, although only extending to four (plus two half) pages, the style was neither in keeping with that of artist-led work of standard Transporter brochures, or the new wave of DDB-inspired work. The cover of the 1959/60 brochure is shown left and that of its successor, the 1960/61 publication, below.

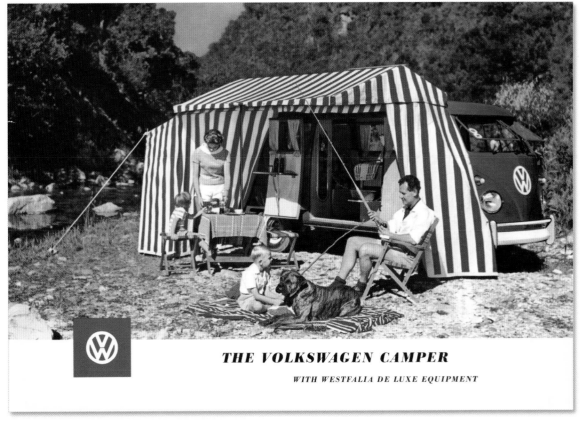

THE VOLKSWAGEN CAMPER

WITH WESTFALIA DE LUXE EQUIPMENT

First produced in 1961, but later revamped, the next generation of VW Camper brochure moved a few steps towards the DDB style, but remained essentially conservative. The size of the brochure remained unaltered, but the number of pages had increased to eight.

The Volkswagen Camper

Ist es eine Jacht?

Despite the absence of a further development in camper design from converters Westfalia, a new VW Camper brochure was issued in 1963, this time with the curious title, "Ist es eine Jacht?" (Is it a yacht?). Showing only part of the vehicle, a glimpse of the side windows and the submarine-style roof hatch were in evidence. From decidedly conservative, DDB had suddenly produced what can only be described as the most unusual, most distinctive brochure of all. In booklet form, the page count rocketed to 16, while the size stood at 288x200mm.

Why, though, was a pelican perched on the roof rack, and why had the person assumed to be the driver a telescope clamped to his left eye? Page-by-page headlines produced a partial answer. "A sidewalk café?", "A clubroom (or playroom)?", "It is a VW Camper Van and it comes in four different models."

Ein Terrassen-Café?

The initial internal spreads of "Ist es eine Jacht?" helped to solve the questions posed by the unusual and thought-provoking cover. "A sidewalk cafe?" (left), "A club (or playroom)?" (below), were followed by a glorious double page spread that announced, "It is a VW Camper Van and it comes in four different models" (bottom).

Ein Clubraum?

DDB's characteristically meaningful but deliberately truncated, almost staccato, text captured any that wavered.

"The Volkswagen Camper isn't a boat. Obviously. But it can take you down to the sea. Or lake. Or river. In fact, the VW camper will go right out on the beach and become your private cabana. Very exclusive ...

"The VW Camper isn't a sidewalk café, either. But it does have atmosphere. Seated under your awning – with a little candlelight, wine, cheese, and a few stars - you could (and can) be anywhere in the world. Very cosmopolitan.

"Of course, the Camper isn't a playroom. But it does have plenty of room for a good game of cards. Or dominoes, or mah-jongg. Or scrabble. With the front seat reversed, there's elbow and sitting room for two, three or even four card players around your 30x20in bridge table. Very fun."

Es ist ein VW-Campingwagen ...

und es gibt ihn in vier verschiedenen Modellen

Eine Jacht ist, wie man sieht, der VW-Campingwagen offensichtlich nicht.
Aber er bringt Sie ans Meer und ins Gebirge. An stille Seen und verträumte Flüsse. Wohin Sie wollen. Und wo es Ihnen gefällt, da können Sie bleiben — solange Sie wollen. Weil Sie frei sind, unabhängig und ungebunden. Weil Ihr privates „Landhaus auf Rädern" haben. Sehr exklusiv und mit vielem Komfort.

Natürlich ist der VW-Campingwagen kein Clubzimmer. Aber er bietet intime Behaglichkeit, Entspannung und wohltuende Ruhe.
Wie angenehm, nach einem Tag reichen Erlebens und Entdeckens mit netten Reisegefährten zu plaudern. Über Land und Leute. (Auch über den VW-Campingwagen?) Für ein gutes Kartenspiel als Tagesabschluß ist Platz genug da: für drei oder sogar für vier Spieler.

Der VW-Campingwagen ist auch kein Terrassen-Café. Aber er hat Atmosphäre.
Er macht den schönen Sommerabend noch schöner. Unter dem großen Vorzelt — mit etwas Kerzenlicht, einem Glas Wein und ein paar Sternen — könnten (und können!) Sie irgendwo in der Welt sein. Abseits der großen Straßen. Fern jeder Hast und jeder Hetze.

Es könnte alles ein schöner Traum sein. Aber es ist keiner.
Es sei denn ein Traum, der in Erfüllung ging ... Der VW-Campingwagen ist Ihr Wohnzimmer, Ihr Speisezimmer oder Ihr Schlafzimmer. Ganz wie Sie es wünschen. — Wünschen Sie mehr über seine verschiedenen Ausführungen zu wissen? Dann lesen Sie bitte die nächsten Seiten.

Uniquely, "Is it a Boat?" was released in two formats, as well as numerous languages. The traditional brochure was supplemented by a fold-out map-style poster, which although it contained slightly less material, when completely opened, measured a near unmanageable 580x396mm. The main image, occupying more than two thirds of one side of the poster, was of the Camper at night, as depicted on the previous page.

Prelude to a story without words

When the next generation of VW Campers emerged in 1965, the part-of-a-vehicle style of cover had more or less disappeared, being replaced by cover images without words.

Although essentially telling the same cover story, the US version of the SO42 Camper brochure used a different image and was smaller in size at 185x185mm. Similarly, the number of pages totalled no more than ten. The reason for the apparent shortfall was that fewer options were offered in the USA.

Both the European and US market SO42 Camper brochures included pages that were simply allocated to photography. The examples reproduced here are from the European version and illustrate the VW Kombi at work during the week (below, left) and as a Camper on a weekend (below, right). The kit, or mosaic, required to achieve this, was not offered in the USA.

A Story without Words

Invariably the practise of producing brochures without text on the cover was restricted to those promoting models already well known by the buying public. The examples reproduced on the following pages are all of that nature. The practice was perpetuated to the end of Nordhoff's life and lingered to through the remaining years of the 1960s, when a self-imposed lack of certainty and direction demanded a change in style.

Above and right, the front and back cover of a 1961 brochure designed to launch the VW 1500. Although examples of VW 1500 launch model brochures have been covered on pages 93 to 96, the version shown here was produced with a different audience in mind. Possibly designed initially for use at the VW 1500's debut at the 1961 Frankfurt Motor International Motor Show, its 52 luxury pages, each lavish in detail and produced entirely of high-quality thin card, were held together by a comb-binder.

It is easy to imagine, although not proven with any degree of certainty that this publication was handed to press and key personnel, plus possibly to many who expressed interest at the various champagne style launches held at subsequent shows and showrooms across the country. Perhaps too, it was with the probability of its use in such circumstances that the decision was taken to remove a title from the front cover and offer a state-of-the-art, ultra-modern looking piece of print.

Schnell und viel auf einmal ... zuverlässig und billig befördern können! Dieses Transport-Problem wurde mit dem VW-Kastenwagen ideal gelöst. Ob Industrie, Handel oder Handwerk: er ist der begehrteste unter allen VW-Transportern. Flott und wendig erledigt er sein tägliches Lieferpensum in schnellem Radumdrehen auch im dichtesten Verkehr. Leicht findet er die passende Parklücke. Und wenn andere vorbeifahren müssen, schlüpft er wie mit dem Schuhlöffel hinein. Selbst auf schlechten Überlandstraßen bringt er 830 kg Transportgut sicher und behutsam ans Ziel. Der 4,8 cbm große Laderaum liegt genau zwischen den Achsen — die empfindlichsten Waren werden schonend befördert. Die seitliche Doppel-Flügeltür ermöglicht es, vom Bürgersteig her gefahrlos und schnell auch massige Lasten einzubringen. So kann der VW-Kastenwagen jederzeit unbehindert beladen und entladen werden, selbst wenn er einmal hinten und vorn von anderen Fahrzeugen eingeengt sein sollte. Die Hecktür — nach oben zu öffnen und feststellbar — bietet weitere bequeme Lademöglichkeiten auch direkt von der Rampe her: das Absetzen von geschulterter Last oder das Einschieben langer Transportgegenstände wird wesentlich erleichtert. Wer von drei Seiten an den Nutzraum heran will, nimmt einen VW-Kastenwagen mit Doppel-Flügeltür an beiden Seiten. Bei einer weiteren Modellvariante, die ebenfalls gegen Mehrpreis geliefert wird, sind im Fahrerabteil an Stelle der dreisitzigen Polsterbank zwei getrennte Sitze eingebaut, wobei die Zwischenwand Kabine-Laderaum entfällt. Die Fracht wird durch den stabilen Ganzstahl-Aufbau geschützt. Scheuerleisten verhüten Schäden

Two brochures without title were published in 1962, each dedicated to the Transporter. The first, 28-page, 295x210mm, was for the home market. The cover (far left) bore a full-frontal view of a red Delivery Van with a uniformed driver behind the wheel. The second, featuring a blue Truck with a more casually dressed driver (left), and set against a deliberately blurred rural background, also had 28 pages, but measured a slightly smaller 272x210mm. Here was another example of one brochure for the European market and another for North America. The US publication depicted the Truck with two-tier bumpers and a style of indicator unit only available on American vehicles at the time. Internal spreads (European market, top, US market, bottom) were similarly the same yet different.

The VW Panel Delivery is roomy enough to make large deliveries practical, yet thrifty enough to make small ones profitable. It can carry 1,830 pounds (⁹/₁₀-ton) in 170 cubic feet of cargo space. ❆ It's remarkably easy to load. Double side doors provide an opening 4 feet by 4 feet; the rear door, which swings up to avoid a traffic hazard, has an opening of over 7 square feet. You could load a ladder through the rear door and a spinet piano through the side door with room to spare. ❆ The load rides smoothly between the axles, in a virtually dustproof, rattle-free, unitized body with sturdy steel-ribbed walls and a corrugated floor. ❆ The most popular of the VW Trucks, the Panel, delivers the goods for thousands of laundries, cleaners, bakeries, food stores, florists, TV repair shops and many other businesses.

Published in 1963, this large 296x210mm untitled brochure told the story of the Micro Bus and Micro Bus De Luxe, with 20 pages containing distinctly clever and informative, or delightfully tongue-in-cheek images (see page 117). The designer allowed the front cover image to occupy two thirds of the rear as well, in order that the vehicle dominated the page without losing the essential atmosphere of its surroundings.

Ihr VW-Händler würde sich freuen, Sie bald zu einer Probefahrt begrüßen zu können

VOLKSWAGENWERK AKTIENGESELLSCHAFT WOLFSBURG

VW Micro Bus

Here's a large touring car for small groups. Or big families. Just as economical as a sedan, but with a lot more room.

All passengers ride comfortably on well padded seat benches. Everybody has plenty of space to stretch out in—there's no luggage in the way. (That's in the roomy compartment in the rear where 16 pieces of hand luggage can be stowed.)

There's excellent visibility all round, thanks to the many windows.

Ventilation and heating systems help to make travelling in a Micro Bus a pleasant pastime.

There's also a seven seater Micro Bus (instead of eight) available on request.

Two persons ride in front, two on the middle seat bench, and three have individual seats.

Late 1963 and the first month of 1964 saw two small-format untitled brochures. The first, a 103x146mm portrait publication (above left), featured the equivalent of a large car park on its cover, the space being filled by every model in Volkswagen's range. Most of the vehicles were occupied by at least a driver. The interior pages contained images of each vehicle in appropriate settings (above).

The second brochure (below left), of virtually the same proportions, featured a photograph of all Volkswagen's commercial vehicles on the cover. Again this came in the form of a car park shot (although taken on a sunnier day) and likewise the interior pages were allocated to examples of each model at work (below).

VW High Roofed Delivery Van

VW Commercials are just the right size (yet another reason for their popularity). In spite of this we have designed this new VW Delivery Van with 13 ins. additional height. Why? So that you can carry even larger, wider and higher things whenever necessary. The VW High Roofed Delivery Van has even more loading space - 212 cu. ft. instead of 170 cu. ft. Its doors are larger too. There is more room to move about and to handle goods. You can even stand upright inside it. What else? Well, it is just as economical and reliable as every VW Commercial, just as manoeuvrable, just as easy to park (so far the parking problem is confined to ground level!) Where else is there plenty of space besides in the van? On the van. Display space for your advertising. Billboard space the same size costs more annually than the whole van.

1965 saw publication of a full-range, full-size brochure without title, with a somewhat abstract image of a hubcap on the cover. Produced on thinner and possibly less expensive paper than was the norm, the brochure's many pages made use of previously seen photographs and often-stunning scenic shots where the car appeared to play a secondary role in the image's composition. These lifestyle pictures, and a section devoted to assembly-line action shots of Beetles at Wolfsburg, compensated for the less lively, text-rich pages elsewhere.

This August 1965 Beetle brochure extended to 48 pages and featured a barely recognisable Beetle hurtling across the sands or a desert. Where it differed from the range brochure was in the minimal amount of text on many pages, coupled to a large font size. In effect, here was the story of the Beetle's suitability for any kind of terrain, told through dramatic photography. Allegedly, London looked like this cart-horse-ridden image in 1966.

A Case Study

Few, if any, other brochures went through four successive covers over a period of years. All told the same story, and all lacked a title.

Version one (left), a 272x210mm landscape brochure of 28 pages including fold-outs, dating from 1962, showed the front of a Ruby Red Delivery Van partially obscured by packing cases. Care had been taken to ensure the large VW roundel on the vehicle's front remained in view, while the back cover continued the theme of packing cases against an indistinct, but clearly industrial, background.

This second edition was a re-orientated version of the first. The same cover image was used on what was now a portrait-style brochure of 30 pages measuring 212x272mm (dimensions shared with its successors). One minor amendment to the cover image (right) was the addition of door mirror, clearly visible to the left.

Another revision was brought about by the introduction, at the start of the 1964 model year in August 1963, of the Transporter with a larger rear window and tailgate. New photography against a different industrial backdrop portrayed the Delivery Van as it had appeared previously on the front cover, but for the first time illustrated the rear of the vehicle, tailgate open, on the back. Rather vthan turn one vehicle to achieve two images, this was a single photograph involving two identical vehicles. However, despite the thought given to showing the Delivery Van at its revised best, one error was made. The vehicles chosen, no doubt pre-series production examples, were still finished in Ruby Red, a colour discontinued at the same time as the larger tailgate was introduced.

The final version (front cover below, left and back cover below, right), dating from 1965 and clearly intended for use during the '66 model year, rectified this oversight. The cover vehicles were now painted in Dove Blue, a colour that had been a key part of the palette from the start of production 15 years earlier. Once again, the background setting had altered.

111

What a Picture, What a Photograph

Stunning, clever, quirky, amusing and informative are just a few of the adjectives that could be applied to much of the photography illustrating the numerous publications issued in the 1960s. The next few pages are dedicated to the finest and encompass all models.

Rundum tipptopp

Der Volkswagen erfüllt eigene Formgesetze. Seine Schönheit lebt nicht vom äußerlichen Zierat, sie liegt in der werterhaltenden Verbindung von zeitloser Eleganz und Vernunft. Darum bleibt die Volkswagen-Karosserie bewußt außerhalb aller kurzlebigen Modeströmungen. Sie richtete sich vom ersten Tage an nach den Regeln der Zweckmäßigkeit und Stabilität. Das ureigene Volkswagengesicht kennt man in der ganzen Welt — es ist ausgeprägt und bleibt doch immer so jung wie der ganze Wagen. Innen wie außen fehlt nichts. Die Sitze (auf Federkern gearbeitet und mit Schaumgummi gepolstert) sind weder bretthart noch ermüdend weich, sondern körpergerecht für die längste Nonstop-Reise. Die beiden Vordersessel lassen sich — auch während der Fahrt — einstellen, wie's der Körper wünscht: zwischen weit nach vorn und ganz zurück, die Lehne steil, mittel oder schräg. Das Volkswagen-Sonnendach (gegen Mehrpreis lieferbar) können Sie ganz weit oder auch nur spaltbreit öffnen, und dazwischen können Sie wählen, ganz wie es Ihnen gefällt. Mit einem Griff stellen Sie das Sonnendach im Fahren beliebig ein. Es ist abwaschbar und unempfindlich. Die feinregulierbare, hochwirksame Heizung sorgt für mollige Wärme. Schwenk- und Kurbelfenster — auf Wunsch und gegen Mehrpreis auch hinten Ausstellfenster — lassen Kühle herein: Sie mischen sich Ihr Klima ganz nach Belieben. Weiterer Vorteil: Der Volkswagen braucht keine Garage. Die Ganzstahl-Karosserie wird im Tauchverfahren grundiert, dann wird die mehrschichtige Hochglanzlackierung eingebrannt — in ihrer Dauerhaftigkeit unübertroffen. Beim Volkswagen erkennt das kritische Auge: Karosserie, Lack, Chrom — dem Teuersten ebenbürtig!

One of several clever images contained with the 1962 publication "Volkswagen 1200". The photographer had found a most effective way to portray the sunroof Beetle's most important asset.

The Volkswagen
is a favourite in 136 countries.

Why?

The 1965 Beetle brochure entitled "The Volkswagen is a favourite in 136 countries. Why?" moves from a stunning cover through 16 pages of cleverly constructed images.

Its purchase price? Low.

How low is low? That depends what you get for your money when you buy a car.

One should ask what's included in the purchase price.

Does it include a fresh air heater for example? A windscreen washer? An ashtray in the rear? A passenger's grab handle? Mounting points for safety belts? Auto-

matic choke? Non-repeat starter ignition switch? Washable plastic roof lining? Folding rear seat backrest? Fully synchronised gearbox? Fuel gauge? Asymmetrical low beam headlights? Foot rests for the passenger? Two swivelling sun vizors?

And this? And that? And the other?

On the Volkswagen all these things are included in the

purchase price.

Why do you think the Volkswagen 1200 has put on 66 lbs. weight since 1959? You are right: because of the many improvements which we have carried out. And the host of extras that we've put on it. That extra weight tells. Very much so when buying a car. Perhaps it even tips the scales.

Answering the question posed on the cover of the brochure on the opposite page through the strap-line and body of text, the photographer took the opportunity to portray a state-of-the-art Volkswagen showroom circa 1965.

Karmann Ghia brochure entitled "Two company? Three a crowd?" from 1967. Copy on the same page illustrates the mood: "Blue skies, the mercury rising. Do you itch to drive an open car?"

The elegant VW 1500 Karmann Ghia Convertible.

Blue skies, the mercury rising. Do you itch to drive an open car? No sooner said than done.

You can put the VW Karmann Ghia's top back in a flash.

Rain, wind, cold, snow? Don't worry. It's just as easy to put the top up again. Then the Convertible is as snug, warm and weather-proof as the Coupé.

The top is heavily padded and is made of a special water-resistant material. It overlaps the windscreen frame and forms a wind and rain-proof seal.

Rear visibility is outstandingly good for a Convertible when the top's up.

Because the rear window is so large.

Wouldn't you like to go places in the exclusive VW 1500 Karmann Ghia Convertible?

For once, the work of photographers Ernst Haas and Dan Budnik was duly credited. Here's the Beetle in Positano, Italy, 1966..

113

A winning setting, care taken to capture the Karmann Ghia's elegant dashboard, and the rather obvious implication that open-top motoring can be achieved in less than a minute. From "Why are some people prepared to pay more for the Karmann Ghia?" 1969.

All about the Volkswagen 1500

Reinforcing the message that this car was just as much a Volkswagen as the Beetle. Perhaps this 1962 cover didn't portray the car in its best light..?

...Fully compensated by spectacular internal page imagery such as this!

Service facilities everywhere for this Volkswagen too

Their good looks are the least important thing about them.

But still, this is no reason to get mad at our competitors. After all, the double-joint rear axle is such a costly affair that, apart from racing cars, it's only found in cars costing a good sight more than the VW. In the Porsche, for example. Or in the Mercedes-Benz.

But, as we said, that's no reason to demand from our competitors that they fit a double-joint rear axle just because we've got one. Let's face it, they have to have a lot of hardware the VW 1600 models don't have to have. (Propeller shaft, radiator, anti-freeze, three yards of exhaust pipe.)

While this 1968 brochure might be entitled "Their good looks are the least important thing about them", internal spreads clearly encompassed appearance against a background of other attributes. The image above right conveys a message relating to the VW 1600's handling abilities, while the text notes characteristics normally restricted to far more expensive cars.

Now can you see yourself in a Volkswagen?

Fastback styling.
Swing-out rear windows.
Louvred air intakes.
Slotted wheel discs.

Cover and enticing page from the August 1969 brochure entitled "Now can you see yourself in a Volkswagen?"

Transporter Ingenuity
Despite the enormous number of photographs depicting the Beetle across the world, it was with the Transporter that designers and photographers won the highest accolades. Brochure after brochure simply oozed ingenuity.

...One of a number of carefully composed images, illustrating the Micro Bus De Luxe's happy fresh-air countenance and its capacity to carry quite a crowd. "Der VW-Kleinbus", 1961.

While the cover image of the 20 page 1963 brochure "How versatile is the VW-Nineseater?" might simply be clever (only the Micro Bus De Luxe featured the very obvious skylight windows), the internal spreads included a variety of lifestyle images, such as the skiing photograph below.

Internal pages (left and below) from the delightful 1963 untitled brochure featured on page 108. The carefully posed photographs illustrated that the Micro Bus was ideal to carry a larger group enjoying a holiday at a splendid hotel, while the comic cowboy and Indian pose of the VW Camper image guarantees even the casual browser's eyes will rest on the page.

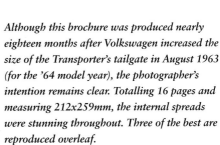

Come potete impiegare in modo redditizio

una Giardinetta VOLKSWAGEN

Although this brochure was produced nearly eighteen months after Volkswagen increased the size of the Transporter's tailgate in August 1963 (for the '64 model year), the photographer's intention remains clear. Totalling 16 pages and measuring 212x259mm, the internal spreads were stunning throughout. Three of the best are reproduced overleaf.

With a title asking how the VW Nine-seater can be used to best advantage (previous page) perhaps it was inevitable that the internal spread photography was devoted to suggestions regarding how this could be achieved.

Portraying the Micro Bus as transport conveying people to and from the airport was a recurrent theme at a time when flying was still largely the prerogative of the well-heeled (top).

In later years, the Range Rover would be portrayed as the ideal vehicle for the hunting, shooting and fishing fraternity. Clearly, Volkswagen wished to define the luxury of the Micro Bus De Luxe as appropriate for those participating in such sports (middle).

Another favourite theme associated with the Micro Bus was one of conveying children from and to school. There was even a publication entitled "Our School Bus". Particularly clever is the blurred foreground, featuring one Micro Bus that frames and attracts the eye towards the second.

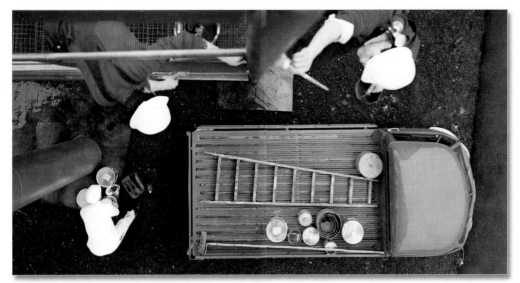

One of a series of inspirational internal pages from the untitled Transporter brochure published in 1965 and featured on page 111. Few would have thought of angling the camera to look down on the Pick-up's most valuable asset, while also composing the picture from a scaffolding viewpoint familiar to many a potential owner, decorators included.

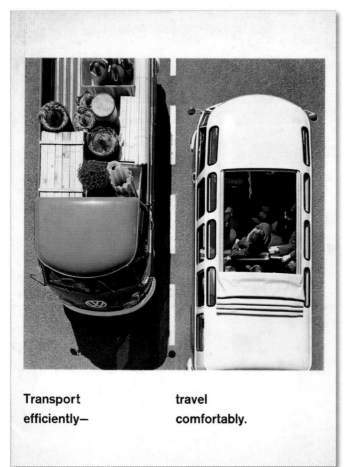

Transport
efficiently—

travel
comfortably.

Transport efficiently.   With the VW Delivery Van.

Transport efficiently.   With the VW Pick-up.

Cover and internal pages of 1965 brochure, "Travel efficiently, travel comfortably". Note how the benefits offered by a Delivery Van with both side loading doors and a rear hatch were highlighted. Similarly, by parking a Pick-up against a warehouse loading bay, the ease with which the vehicle can be either loaded or unloaded is instantly apparent.

Various titles were attributed to the late 1960s and early 1970s brochure, ranging from a straightforward "Die VW Transporter" for the German market and "Volkswagen Trucks. For the cost conscious" in Canada, who also arranged for the vehicle on the cover to be repainted red. All versions extended to many pages – the example reproduced here had 36 – and each carried a full series of images depicting each Transporter in a role suited to its particular purpose. Thus here, the High Roofed Delivery Van (top right) was to be loaded with clothes that could hang without touching the floor and creasing. Similarly, the VW Pick-up with enlarged platform (bottom left) was ideally suited to carrying vegetables for market. The load was light, yet bulky. How many additional crates could be loaded without detriment thanks to the wide platform? Finally (bottom right) the theme of conveying people in luxury to the airport through the use of a Micro Bus De Luxe, (now known as the Microbus L) is a familiar one.

The Commercial for the Cost Conscious.

The VW High Roofed Delivery Van

It has a 219 cu. ft. load compartment, a 44.1 sq. ft. load surface and a payload of up to 2039 lbs.

The VW Pick-Up with enlarged platform

It has a 56.2 sq. ft. load surface and a payload of up to 2028 lbs.

The VW Microbus L

With 212 cu. ft. inside.
35 cu. ft. of which is luggage space.

Anyone for Snakes and Ladders?

It's only possible to scratch the surface of the mountain of literature produced for and by Volkswagen. The two pieces of material reproduced here cannot be missed, although they don't fit any of the categories determined as hallmarks of the DDB style of the decade.

The first was small (204x140mm), consisted of just two sides, lacked full colour and was released for the US market in 1959. "Here are the SAVINGS on just one mile," shouted the headline. Sure enough, they were. Attached to the reverse were seven real cents! The copywriter had worked out that the cost of running a, "usual truck" was, "about fourteen cents per mile," while those of the VW averaged half that figure. The message was in the final line of copy. "Figure out how much you would save in a year - then let's talk over the rest of the exciting economy-and-performance story of Volkswagen Trucks."

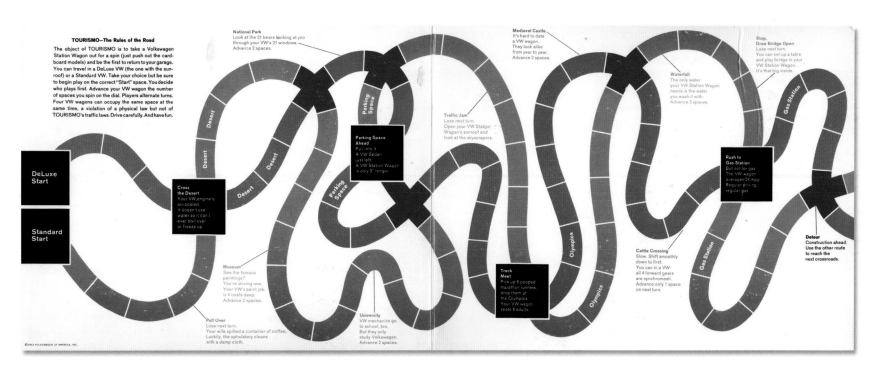

"Tourismo", Volkswagen of America's Station Wagon sight-seeing game, copyrighted in 1963, was a bit of fun with a serious purpose (to sell more Station Wagons, of course). Measuring 283x214mm and printed on board, Tourismo folded out, in the best tradition of any board game, to a lengthy route from start to finish of 1132mm (over four pages). Push-out trucks replaced counters, while advances and negatives, just like the average snakes-and-ladders game, littered the road. Amazingly, the negatives also exhibited positives – and everyone bought a VW and lived happily ever after!

Moving on

The death of Heinz Nordhoff in April 1968 marked a turn in the Volkswagen's propects. His successor appeared to have little regard for the cars that had made Volkswagen a fortune. At around this time a new phase in brochure advertising was beginning to emerge. The style was plain and straightforward, an approach for European markets appreciated by many a contemporary designer for its bold colour and its very simplicity, but not much favoured by fans of 1950s' artwork and clever 1960s' photography and copy.

While it is possible to locate brochures of a plain and simple style dating from the early- and mid-years of the 1960s, as the front pages of Volkswagen Standard-Limousine (1962, shown left) and the VW-Kleinlieferwagen (1965, shown right) illustrate, such material was in a minority. Probably, the VW 1500 was the first range to experience elements of change. Gone were the eye-catching half-vehicles of old and, by the time of the debut of the twin-carburettor VW 1500S in August 1963, much plainer brochure covers (opposite bottom), with interiors to match, were on dealers' shelves.

However, it was with the launch of the second-generation Transporter, and the Beetle with vertically-set headlamps and girder-profile bumpers, both in the summer of 1967, that the new style became truly apparent.

With a near-fluorescent pink cover and nothing more than the words, "The New Beetle" (in mismatched orange-red) splattered across the page, both the car and the latest take on a plain style of promotion hit Europe (page 124). Amid the splash of colour, a key statement might have been lost: the car was no longer the Volkswagen; at last it was the Beetle!

Inside, the 30 pages of this oversized 235x325mm brochure were arresting, if simple. Stark, eye-catching imagery stood side-by-side with big print but less than zippy text. Two more editions, featuring equally striking splashes of colour on the cover, were released throughout Europe during 1968. Shocking pink was succeeded by liquid lime green, which in turn gave way to the most palatable of the bunch, imperial purple with a hint of mint!

Virtually in tandem with the new look for the revitalised Beetle, loud covers proclaimed the arrival of the second-generation Transporter (page 125). The rich peacock blue cover of the 46-page 210x295mm brochure found its way to Volkswagen's many markets.

While the covers of this array of brochures had more of a story to tell than the Beetle version, the internal pages were somewhat disappointing. Sadly, photography was neither stunningly simple nor beguiling, but rather distinctly plain, bordering on dull. Conversely, a fold-out near the beginning and a double-headed affair at the brochure's centre hinted at a lavishness the photographs failed to convey. As for the copy, its strength lay in the slightly offbeat headlines and a body largely devoid of detail.

Come August 1969, this latest style of Transporter brochure was shipped across the Atlantic, where it was adopted by Volkswagen of Canada under the heading, "The big one". However, this was not entirely a lock, stock and barrel transplant, as the headlines and copy confirmed.

Leaflet for the Standard Beetle, 1962.

Volkswagen
Standard-Limousine
DM 4200,– a. W.

Volkswagen 1200 Limousine
Standard-Modell:
Jetzt mit hydraulischer Vierradbremse.
Nur DM 4200,– ab Werk.

Der preisniedrigste Volkswagen überhaupt –
mit allen Vorzügen des Export-Modells:
gleiche Wirtschaftlichkeit und lange Lebensdauer.
Gleiche Sicherheit und Zuverlässigkeit.
Wie bei jedem Volkswagen:
Heckmotor und Luftkühlung. Kein Kühlwasser.
Kein Gefrierschutzmittel. Keine Garagensorgen.
Nichts kann kochen im Sommer
oder einfrieren im Winter.

Volkswagen-Standard-Limousine – ein Wagen,
den sich jeder leisten kann!

VW-Kleinlieferwagen

VOLKSWAGENWERK AG · WOLFSBURG

The two-page brochure of 1965 vintage dedicated to the recently introduced VW-Kleinlieferwagon, literally the small delivery van, was a simple affair. Its style was in keeping with leaflets describing the merits of special models and in reality, this is what the vehicle was. Clearly, there was little point in DDB creating a glossy brochure full of both enticing imagery and inspirational text. Nicknamed the Fridolin (tiny toddler, a name bestowed on small German boys), this vehicle had been designed as a concept at the request of the Deutsche Bundespost.

Four Volkswagens in the 1.5 Litre Class

As the 1960s developed a small percentage of brochures were offered with this simple, even plain, style of cover. Strictly the preserve of European market material, this particular 1963 brochure was designed to coincide with the introduction of the twin carburettor VW 1500S.

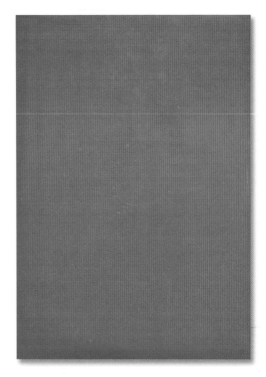

The summer of 1967 and a new breed of Beetle was promoted by a new plain but striking style of brochure. Such material, although originated by DDB, was exclusive to European markets.

Außen:
Zwar etwas verändert.
Aber immer noch der Käfer.

Zum Tanken braucht nicht die vordere Haube geöffnet zu werden: Der Tankeinfüllstutzen ist rechts außen hinter einer Klappe. Diese Klappe kann nur vom Wageninneren aus geöffnet werden.

Die Tankklappe ist jetzt verriegelt

Der Türgriff hat keinen Druckknopf, sondern eine innenliegende Zugtaste. Dadurch haben Sie mehr Sicherheit gegen ein Aufspringen der Türen. Auch die Fronthaube ist durch einen Sicherheitsknopf gegen ein Aufspringen gesichert.

Die vordere Haube und die Motorhaube sind so gebaut, daß man sie auch dann noch öffnen kann, wenn die Stoßstangen mal eingedrückt werden sollten.

Türgriff mit innenliegender Zugtaste statt Druckknopf

Was freilich recht schwer ist. Denn vorn wie hinten sind die Stoßstangen breit und kräftig geworden. Außerdem sind sie hoch angebracht.

Die Scheinwerfer sind weit vorgezogen und haben senkrechte Streuscheiben. Das gibt eine gute Ausleuchtung der Fahrbahn.

Scheinwerfer mit senkrechter Streuscheibe

Breite und kräftige Stoßstangen

The interior pages of the new style of Beetle brochure were striking due to their simplicity. The large format (most examples measured up to 235x254mm), the quantity of pages (totalling 32), stark imagery and large font text, all contributed to the brochures' appeal.

And it's still just as economical as a Volkswagen.

Whether you drive it like this . . .

or like this – you can always be sure of one healthy item in your accounts.

Even if you're making a run which of itself is pretty uneconomical. With only a small carton as load, for example. Or with nothing at all.
How come? Because the running costs are still as low as ever. Which means that all the mileage covered empty or semi-empty doesn't make all that much difference. Logically enough, the converse is also true. The mileage covered fully laden makes a great deal of difference. To the credit side of your bank balance. And after all, 177 cu. ft. is 177 cu. ft.!

The new VW Clipper has passenger car comfort.

And even then some. Just you try and find a passenger car with as much space for you and your passengers.
And try and find one in this price bracket with more comfortably upholstered seats.
Or, for example, how many passenger cars do you know of which have a sliding door and which are so easy to get into? Or which have so many windows – and such large ones?
And how many passenger cars do you know of with a 35.3 cu. ft. luggage compartment? But we've taken things even further.

Three covers from brochures designed to promote the second generation Transporter – January 1968, January 1969 and January 1970.

Sadly, the interior pages of the new style of brochure for European and other market Transporters didn't match the crisp nature of the design of the covers. Fortunately, at least for a few more years, this type of brochure was not the only one to be stocked by the dealers.

THE 1970S

August 1970 saw the launch of the 1302, a very different kind of Beetle, to head the range. By coincidence, it was also from this point that the stark, plain cover theme of 1967 quickly flooded all European markets. Just as the 1302 (and its curved-screen successor of two years later) was loathed by traditionalists, so too admirers of Volkswagen's advertising found it hard to adapt.

Although one or two other Beetle brochures intended for consumption across Europe still existed, by far the most dominant was an offering with a plain yellow cover broken only by a simple, if varying, title. The exception to the rule, not in words but in cover format, was the home-market brochure. The title, "Die Käfer" (The Beetles) sat neatly in a

August 1970 cover - Beetle, Dutch market.

yellow band across the top of the cover, but the rest was given over to a frontal image of the new 1302 Beetle. The photograph had been taken on a dreary winter's day!

Inside these 1970 brochures, not only did the number of pages vary (36 in Germany, 32 in the Netherlands, 28 in Britain and 28 in Sweden) but also the order in which the models were presented. Commonality of imagery was not universal either, with each market seemingly being offered at least one image thought most appropriate to its potential customers. Most of the photographs were reasonably dramatic, although a trend towards tinting and less-than-pin-sharp photography might have disappointed some dealers.

One year later, in August 1971, the plain yellow cover was

Daar komen de Kevers!

A typical example of the dramatic, but not always terribly clear, photography used across the internal spreads of the 1970 Beetle brochures.

Die Käfer

While the German home market Beetle brochure for August 1970 featured a picture on the cover, a drab winter's day was deemed satisfactory to promote the top-of-the-range Beetle.

Aber wir haben auch diese Käfer verbessert.

August 1970 – and more, sometimes reused, challenging interior spreads.

replaced by a smallish frontal image of the car set against a black background, while the title was presented in bigger and bolder letters. Both were set against yellow, the colour chosen to represent the Beetle, just as varying shades of mauve/purple would signify the Transporter, a definite orange the Karmann Ghia and so on. The inclusion of an image of a vehicle on the cover was not set to last. Completely plain covers had enveloped Volkswagen's European brochures by 1973.

The apparent desire for uniformity soon extended to internal pages. Instantly noticeable was the commonality of text, and nowhere more so than on the first two pages. On the left was the name of the vehicle and on the right a series of headings. In 1971, the Beetle version announced that potential purchasers should, "See it. Drive it. Choose it. Own it. Love it." Quite soon a rather important sixth message, suggesting customers, "Buy it," had been added.

The Beetle.

August 1971 cover – Beetle, British market.

European market Beetle brochures dating from August 1971 and later featured the welcome return of the cutaway drawing. Although intended to illustrate the design improvements associated with the new MacPherson-strut 1302 Beetle, the cutaway acted as a welcome respite from pages designed to a template.

Drive the Beetle – to see what makes it tick.

The fact that outside all Beetles look very much alike cannot hide the fact that today's Beetle is far more technically advanced than any in the past.

To mention only a few of the technical advances made in the construction of the Beetle in the last few years:

It's equipped with a dual circuit brake system which brakes even if one system is out of action (though that's hardly likely to happen). A semi-trailing arm rear axle which makes for particularly safe cornering. And you can get it with an Automatic which was specially developed for the Beetle.

But the improvements don't stop there. The Super Beetle now has a new front axle configuration. Which enlarges the luggage space. And reduces the turning circle.

It's much quieter too. Better engine suspension insulates the differential and the gearbox from the chassis. And there's less resonance from vibrations from the road.

Our engineers have definitely not forgotten the air we breathe. A lot of changes have been made to the ignition and intake systems to ensure that exhaust fumes comply with all the regulations. But don't think that pure air is paid for by a poor engine and reduced output.

Interior double-page spread illustrating performance, useful luggage space and additional ventilation details.

Drive the Beetle – and enjoy the comfort.

The Beetle is economical. Which doesn't mean though that we skimped on comfort.

On the contrary. It's a pleasure to drive the Beetle, and a pleasure to drive in it.

The driver has a pleasant feeling of being one with the road. Its big wheels are all independently sprung. And now there's more of the road to be seen in the rear-view mirror through the enlarged rear window. An added pleasure.

Passengers will appreciate the efficiency of the flow-through ventilation system, which constantly but unobtrusively replaces stale air with fresh. And the cosy atmosphere, both

front and back. They'll enjoy the comfort of the soft upholstery. And the fact that now there's even less irritating noise inside than ever before.

Add to this the coat hooks, assist straps, 85% more luggage space up front in the Super Beetle, a shelf that keeps the luggage hidden too, the roomy glove box — and you have all the comfort you'd expect to find in a luxury saloon.

In the Beetle it's a matter of course. And the price of the extras you extra specially want you'll find are kept extra specially low.

Template text began to engulf the Transporter and other models as the 1970s started to gather pace. While the attributes of different models may have varied, the copywriter had to engineer his words to fit rigid guidelines on the number of words per page and specific headings. The result was clean and succinct, but hardly inspirational.

As an example, "De VW Kleinbus. Bekijken, besturen, kiezen, bezitten, waarderen, kope" (The VW Microbus. View, choose, possess, control, appreciate, buy) was the announcement on pages two and three of the Micro Bus brochure for the Netherlands in August 1972. In Britain, a publication bearing the same date, but covering all models in the Transporter range, offered browsers the message "See it. Drive it. Choose it. Have it. Respect it. Buy it".

De VW-kleinbus bekijken. Al aan de | **buitenkant ziet hij er uitnodigend uit.**

En wel omdat hij in kleuren voor geen enkele personenauto onder doet. En omdat hij zo handig en compact van omvang is als geen andere vergelijkbare auto. En ook, omdat hij nog mooier geworden is.
Het eerste wat opvalt aan zijn nieuwe gezicht is de sterkere bumper. (Aan de achterkant zit er

nog zo een.) In de L-uitvoering zijn ze voorzien van praktische zwarte rubberstrips. Bovendien is er een speciaal element in aangebracht met dezelfde eigenschappen als een kreukelzone. Het is een verzachtende omstandigheid, mocht u ooit ergens tegen aan botsen.

De clignoteurs zitten nu op een betere plaats: naast het luchtrooster. En de treeplanken liggen nu binnen de wagen: dat ziet er moderner uit. Mensen die ermee mogen of moeten rijden, vinden hem zeer uitnodigend. Ook omdat ze, zelfs als ze flink uit de kluiten gewassen zijn, gemak-

kelijk door de royale schuifdeur kunnen in- en uitstappen. En ook omdat ze op het eerste gezicht wel kunnen zien dat hij zijn inzittenden niet hotsend en botsend zal vervoeren.
En vergeet niet, dat deze reusachtige personenauto op elke normale parkeerplaats past. Ook dat is tegenwoordig een groot pluspunt.

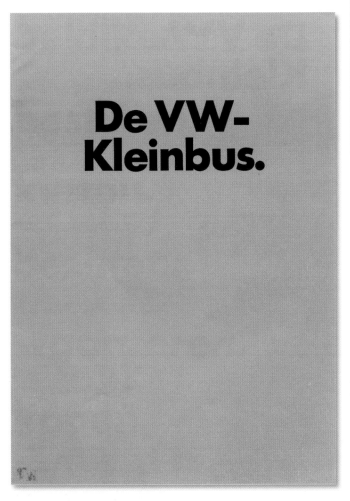

August 1972 cover – Micro Bus,
German home market.

1971 and the age of individuality for Transporter brochure design, as far as Europe was concerned, was more-or-less over. On the plus side, the photography was simple and clear, while the accompanying text was succinct.

De VW-kleinbus kiezen. Voor 7 of 8 | **personen, in standaard- of luxe uitvoering.**

De VW-Kleinbus is een acht-persoonsauto in twee uitvoeringen: standaard en luxe. De standaarduitvoering is erg comfortabel, de luxenog meer.
Die is ook wat mooier. Door een sierstrip die om de hele auto heen loopt, door het spuiten in twee kleuren, door de (ook praktische) rubber strips op de bumpers, door de sierlijst om het

luchtrooster en door het verchroomde VW-embleem.
Het extra comfort bestaat uit o.a. een schuifdak, een snelheidsmeter met dagkilometerteller, een klok en bouclébekleding in de bagageruimte.
U ziet, het is één en al luxe in de luxe-uitvoering.

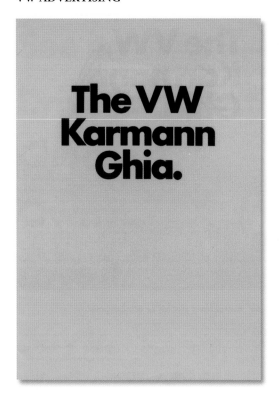

Cover, August 1972 – Karmann Ghia,
British market.

Double page spread, Karmann
Ghia, August 1972.

Choose the Karmann Ghia. Two individual ways to top it.

Here's a sight you won't see often. Two Volkswagen Karmann Ghias.

In this age of mass production, cars like the Karmann Ghia are few and far between.

Ghia the Italian designer dreamt it up. Karmann the German coach-builder turned the dream into reality. So it's designed and built by craftsmen. And because it's a car for discerning people they take their time with every one.

Each body panel is a perfectly tailored fit. Joined by hand-welded, hand-filled seams, hand-smoothed until they're out of sight.

And if all this individual attention isn't enough, we can get you the convertible model. With a hood that takes two craftsmen four hours to tailor by hand. So it fits like a glove.

Cover, August 1970 – VW 1600,
British market.

Outside.

The VW 1600s are famous for their reliability, quality and durability. After all, we've been making them since 1961. And practice makes perfect.

Last year, for the first time, we changed their looks.

We made the front end nearly 5 inches longer. The whole car looks leaner, racier. Good, the extra inches made the VW 1600s look better. But the important thing is that they also made them safer. The passenger compartment is designed as a safety cell, whereby the front and rear ends act as so-called crumple zones. The more there is to crumple, the safer the car.

And, of course, the front luggage compartment was made larger in the process. Together with the rear luggage compartment – now also larger thanks to a modified parcel shelf – the Fastback has a total luggage capacity of 19.3 cu.ft.

Last year, we made the VW 1600s longer and more attractive. This year, we've made a number of practical improvements.

Take a look at the bottom picture on this page, for example. Yes, that's right, those funny looking slits. They're part of the flow-through ventilation system. If you care to turn over, we'll tell you how it works.

VW 1600 TE Fastback

The car in action and detail
shots... Seen it all before.

Some might have suggested that in creating such universal templates, Volkswagen's advertising gurus were unconsciously confirming what less-careful managers had made public, namely that the air-cooled story was fast running out of breath. But this was clearly not the case. Why?

Because brochures for the VW Passat (1973), VW Scirocco and VW Golf (1974) and the VW Polo (1975) simply mirrored those of their air-cooled ancestors and would do for a number of years to come. This was the style of the era, like it or loathe it!

More of the same. A common design policy for all models.

December 1970 cover for the VW 411LE, British market.

The VW 411LE is as comfortable as they come. And more so.

You'll soon see that there's a great deal more to it than meets the eye — or than the elegant simplicity of its lines would lead you to suspect.

Take the instrument panel, for example. Padded top and bottom. And with pliable plastic control knobs. Easy to reach and impossible to confuse.

And then there's the electronically controlled heating system. This is how it works.

You simply set it to the temperature you want — and forget about it. The temperature remains constant. It makes no difference how fast you're going. Or whether the engine's on or off.

Fresh air is supplied by a fully adjustable, flow-through ventilation system — complete with two-speed blower.

There's a windscreen washer and good big windscreen wipers. Two-speed and self-parking, of course.

The front seats would do many a more expensive car proud as well. They're adjustable, not only backwards and forwards but up and down as well.

And they're not just adjustable forwards to make room for the back seat passengers either. Not even the longest legs get short shrift in the VW 411 LE.

And then there are a whole range of other "little" details.

Fully reclining seats, for example. Just the thing if you feel like taking a nap en route.

The VW 411 LE has parking lights, rubber strips on the bumpers, stainless steel trim mouldings at the waistline, on the gutterings and around the wheel housings.

It has an electric clock in the instrument panel and carpeting on the floor.

Just by way of example.

The VW 411 LE. As we said, it's the little details which make all the difference.

VW 411 LE

Cover, 1979 – Transporter, British market.

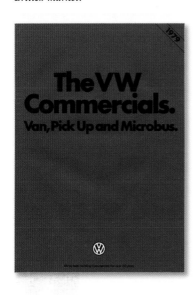

The VW Commercials.
Van, Pick Up and Microbus.

There was deliberately little change in style from the early years of the 1970s to the end of the decade.

The VW Commercial: Sound commercial sense.

The Volkswagen Commercials, a whole range of vans, pick-ups and buses that are as tough as the transport business itself.

We've been building Commercials for over 28 years. But we've never got complacent. Every year we try and improve them. Today's Commercial is a perfect blend of passenger car comfort and commercial toughness and with over 4¼ million sales is the world's best selling commercial in its class. Its reputation speaks for itself.

The basic forward control concept, envied and copied by so many combines the minimum overall dimensions (the Commercials only 14'9" long) with the maximum internal dimensions. The unitary body construction combines strength with low weight for maximum payload.

The combined engine and four speed synchromesh transmission unit mounted in the rear over the driving wheels, gives lightweight and maximum traction.

The fully independent torsion bar suspension all round combines toughness with ride comfort to handle any load and to keep the driver comfortably in control.

Choose from the frugal standard 1.6 litre (50 b.h.p.) or the powerful 2.0 litre (70 b.h.p.) engines and you have all the advantages of air cooled engines. They won't boil or freeze and have no water hoses, radiator or water pump to let you down. The larger engine has

brake servo and radial ply tyres as standard and is also available with manual or automatic transmission.

Choose a VW Commercial and you also choose a fully trimmed cab, passenger seat, sliding side loading door (van models) and factory finished gloss paint because they all come as standard equipment.

That VW symbol on the front isn't just for looks. It means something; reliability, durability, economy and quality.

2

3

131

With a simple red cover bearing the words "The VW 1600s" the 1970 20-page brochure for the Type 3 behind the scenes, seemed to obey all the latest template rules. However, as a cutaway drawing wasn't available, one transgression was apparent in the form of a photograph of the chassis coupled to reassuring text.

Few cars are as well-made, reliable and as advanced as the VW 1600s. Or as safe.

Let's start with the chassis.

The VW 1600s have large 15" wheels with independent suspension and springing. (There's no more of this business of one wheel passing the buck on to its opposite number.) The VW 1600s keep all four feet on the ground at all times.

The drive wheels are firmly kept in place by the weight of the air-cooled engine at the back. (Makes them less likely to go into a spin — invaluable on icy roads.)

And then, of course, the VW 1600s come fitted with one of the most up-to-date bits of axle design on the market — the semi-trailing arm rear axle with double-joint drive shafts. Expensive, true. But worth it. The VW 1600s corner like thoroughbreds. Because the axle gives the wheels outstanding lateral stability.

Further safety is provided by the safety steering column which collapses on impact. And, of course, by the brakes — self-adjusting disc brakes up front and large drum brakes at the back. Fast-acting brakes coupled to a dual circuit brake line system.

You can still pull up even if one circuit fails. (Which virtually never happens.)

Cover and internal two page spread for "La Hormiga" (an attempt to offer an economy version of the Transporter), 1977. No model was excluded from the uniform approach in presentation.

La Hormiga.

La hormiga, infatigable transporte económico de carga.

La hormiga es la más reciente creación de la ingeniería Volkswagen: un infatigable, resistente y económico transporte para carga, cuyo nombre fue inspirado por los laboriosas hormigas del reino animal.

Resuelve un gran número de problemas y necesidades de transporte de carga en zonas urbanas, suburbanas y rurales, por lo que tiene múltiples aplicaciones en el comercio, la industria y el campo.

Durante su planeación se estudiaron y tomaron en cuenta factores humanos, técnicos y económicos, a fin de hacer de la hormiga un útil y ligero vehículo, práctico y muy resistente.

Por su funcional diseño y sólida construcción, la hormiga despliega una gran capacidad de trabajo. Su amplia plataforma le permite transportar una tonelada de carga, sin importar el volumen de la misma.

El económico motor de la hormiga, de 1,600 c.c., va colocado al centro del vehículo para darle una adecuada distribución de peso.

El interior de la cabina de la hormiga le sorprenderá por su amplitud, ya que en ella viajan cómodamente el conductor y dos ayudantes. Y para tener aun mayor seguridad, cuenta con tres cinturones pélvicos de dos puntos de apoyo. Su gran parabrisas y sus ventanillas laterales y trasera, ofrecen una visibilidad panorámica.

La hormiga es un vehículo creado con el único fin de serle útil, proporcionándole la forma más económica de transportar carga.

The VW
181.

*The 1973 VW 181 brochure seemingly didn't
warrant a coloured cover, but the internal
pages carried the same design style.*

The VW 181 — an all-purpose Volkswagen.

Wherever roads stop being roads, wherever getting through is a must, no matter how tough the going, that's where the VW 181 really shows its mettle. An all-round car that is always fun to drive no matter why one's driving it. This is the car that gives you the advantage of Volkswagen's experience with millions of other cars. Cars that have gone through thick and thin all over the world. Over steppes and through jungles. Across hot deserts in the south. And through the ice-cellars of the north. From stem to stern, the VW 181 was designed for versatility. For miners and farmers. Roadbuilders and foresters.

It is what they need for their tough work. The Acapulco version of the VW 181 is the ideal vehicle for tourist companies, airports, hotels and safari centres. And for the numerous holidaymakers, who have not brought their own car with them: a welcome, breezy, leisuretime change. This extraordinary multi-purpose car is very popular with sportsmen too. Fishermen or gliding buffs, golfers and skiers. It makes itself useful everywhere. For those who want a solid roof over their heads in winter, there's the additional hardtop available for the standard VW 181. This white plastic top is just as easy to manage as the convertible top. It fastens on in the same way and can carry a weight of about 110 lbs. A great variety of additional extras are available for all versions of the VW 181.

What might have been...

Transporter brochures such as "The New One" and "The Big One" had made their mark before the 1960s had drawn to a close, but for the briefest of periods there was a possibility that an alternative style to the plain covers might successfully emerge. Spearheading the alternative campaign has to be a brochure such as March 1970's "We make the VW Microbus for all sorts of people". With a cover lacking any sign of a Volkswagen but illustrating a spectrum of human types, the first pages carried headlines reminding readers who the VW Micro Bus was designed to accommodate. "For people who drive it... For people who are driven in it... For people who never drive it," the last being a clever way of highlighting use by airlines, hotels and the like.

Before finally succumbing to a plain green cover in its final incarnation, what had been originally, "Der Transporter für Leute, die immer nur ans Geschäft denken" had become plain "Die VW-Transporter" by 1970. Otherwise, this brochure was full of intriguingly clever photography.

Der VW-Personentransporter

Nicht umsonst ist der VW-Personentransporter der meistgefahrene der Welt.

Was müssen das für Leute sein, die den VW-Personentransporter fahren?

Vernünftige Leute.

Die, die ihn geschäftlich fahren. Und die, die ihn privat fahren.

Fangen wir mit denen an, die immer nur ans Geschäft denken. Das sind oftmals Dienstleistungsbetriebe wie Fluggesellschaften, Reiseunternehmer, Hotels und Städtische Verwaltungen. Und es sind Architekten, Bauunternehmer, Fußball- und Sportvereine, Wagenvermietungen, Handelsvertreter, Kindergärten, usw.

Zu der anderen Gruppe gehören Privatleute aus allen Schichten, denen es Spaß macht, eine außergewöhnliche Limousine zu fahren, die praktisch alle und alles mitnimmt, was man so hat. Sieben Kinder und eine Frau zum Beispiel. (In Amerika wird er sogar mehr und mehr von Hausfrauen als Zweitwagen gefahren. Vor allem aus Platz- und Sicherheitsgründen.)

Wer ihn auch fährt, über die Vorteile des VW-Personentransporters sind sich alle einig. Denn er ist billig in der Anschaffung. Hat geringe Betriebs- und Kilometerkosten. Einen hohen Gegenwert. Eine lange Lebensdauer. Und alles, was man vom Volkswagen zum Volkswagen macht.

Die sprichwörtliche VW-Wirtschaftlichkeit. Die VW-Zuverlässigkeit. Und die VW-Qualität.

"Die VW-Transporter" spawned two siblings, August 1970's "Der VW-Personentransporter" and "Der VW Campingwagen" of February 1971, both featuring the finest in appealing and thought-provoking images. Sadly, such material was quickly and totally eclipsed.

Der VW-Campingwagen

So wohnen Sie.

Wo immer Sie mit Ihrem VW-Campingwagen anhalten und wohnen, werden Sie es gemütlich haben. Denn so sachlich und kompakt der VW-Campingwagen in seiner äußeren Form ist, so gemütlich und geräumig ist er innen.

Eine 25 mm dicke Silan-Schicht isoliert den Innenraum gegen Temperaturschwankungen und Lärm. Sie ist mit hellem Birkenholz verkleidet.

Aus Naturholz mit Kunststoff-Furnier sind auch die Einrichtungsgegenstände, die alle fest mit dem Fahrzeug verbunden sind. Der Fußboden ist mit einer filzbeschichteten PVC-Folie ausgelegt. Darunter sorgt eine Sperrholzplatte für Isolation von unten.

Alle Polstergarnituren sind wahlweise mit strapazierfähigem Stoff oder Schaum-Kunstleder bezogen. Am Tisch haben gut vier Personen Platz. Zum Schlafen schwenkt man ihn einfach weg. Und zieht rundherum die bunten Gardinen vor. Als Lichtquelle dient dann eine 12 V-Deckenleuchte (10-30 Watt).

Wenn Sie mit einem VW-Campingwagen unterwegs sind, brauchen Sie keine Koffer ein- und auszupacken. Denn Kleider, Wäsche und Geschirr sind geordnet und griffbereit in verschiedenen Schränken und Stauräumen untergebracht.

So schlafen Sie.

Mit ein paar Handgriffen machen Sie aus Ihrem Wohnraum einen Schlafraum. Zuerst wird die hintere Sitzbank nach vorn gezogen. Dabei legt sich die Rücklehne flach. Zusammen mit dem Polster, das über dem Motorraum liegt, entsteht ein bequemes Doppelbett. Darin können sich selbst zwei große Erwachsene in ihrer vollen Länge ausstrecken. Die Breite des Bettes richtet sich danach, wieviel Schränke Sie eingebaut haben.

Das Bettzeug hat tagsüber im Stauraum unter der Polsterbank seinen Platz.

In einem VW-Campingwagen haben Sie mehr Schlafgelegenheiten, als Sie denken.

Im Fahrerhaus können Sie über den Sitzen ein Hängebett für ein kleineres Kind befestigen.

Im Ausstelldach gibt es ein Faltbett für einen Erwachsenen, der nicht größer als 1,70 m ist, oder für ein Kind (in einer Ausstattungsvariante sogar für zwei Kinder).

Und im Faltdach sind zwei Erwachsenenbetten.

Das heißt also, daß Sie mit einem VW-Campingwagen alles in allem ein Hotel für vier Erwachsene und ein Kind haben.

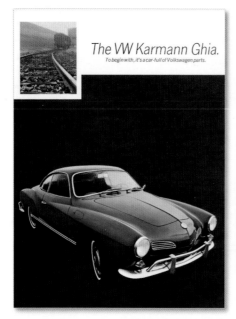

So Many Improvements they are Beginning to Show

Whereas European-market brochures of the 1970s lost the quirky ingenuity of the previous decade, becoming strait-laced in design and low key in their message, in the USA and elsewhere the tap continued to flow.

Take, for example, the Karmann Ghia. From 1967 to 1968, the North American Karmann Ghia brochure told the car's story from the arrival of Volkswagen components at the Karmann factory, through the various stages of manufacture, to everyday use. The psychology was, of course, that the car was a handcrafted masterpiece at an affordable price, using trustworthy Volkswagen components.

From 1969 through to 1971, the US Karmann brochure cover posed the question, "Is it really a sports car?". From a starting point suggesting that it was, the headings changed to imply the opposite, and the conclusion was open-ended: "Sports cars have racy, hand-finished bodies. So does the Karmann Ghia... Sports cars have tight, road-holding suspension. So does the Karmann Ghia... Sports cars need specialised service. The Karmann Ghia doesn't... Sports cars cost a lot of money. The Karmann Ghia doesn't... The VW Karmann Ghia. Is it really a sports car? That depends on how you look at it."

In 1972 and 1973, what had been a question became a statement: "The Karmann Ghia. Our Idea Of A Sports Car." The images were was just as intriguing and inspirational, while the copy was miles ahead in terms of readability compared to equivalent European-market material. The copy might have been self-deprecating, but in a way that was always to Volkswagen or Karmann's advantage. "Take away the Karmann Ghia's beautiful Italian designed body and what have you got? A sports car that's as reliable as a Volkswagen."

Even as Wolfsburg was desperately trying to rid itself of the Karmann Ghia, the American market brochure for 1974 still had a story to tell. Reduced to just four pages, it wasn't particularly lavish, but there was no implication of loss of interest, or of desperately trying to sell an end-of-line.

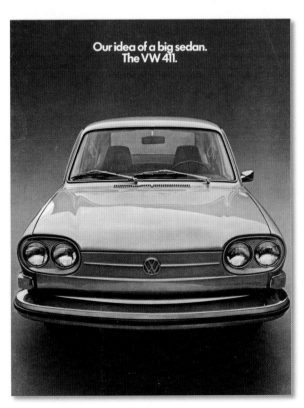

Perhaps the most potent example of genuine belief in the product came with the VW411 and its successor the VW412, dating from 1972 and 1973. Our idea of a big sedan – the VW 411 declared, "They come with extras you'd expect to pay extra for in a big car," and concluded: "You won't have to decide which big car to buy. Just which 411."

By 1973, it was luxury all the way. From the cover's "The VW 412 – a luxury you can afford", the pages unfolded: "Luxury is being able to buy a big car that's built with the craftsmanship of a Volkswagen... Luxury is driving a car that's engineered so well only a Rolls-Royce warranty lasts longer... Luxury is a car so technologically advanced it can give itself a thorough check-up."

Now can you see yourself in a Volkswagen?

Computerized fuel injection.
Aluminum-magnesium engine.
Front-wheel disc brakes.
Four-speed synchromesh transmission
or fully-automatic transmission.

Electronic fuel injection.
Magnesium-aluminum engine.
Front-wheel disc brakes.
Four-speed synchromesh transmission.
Or optional fully automatic transmission.

A facelift for the VW 1600, introduced to coincide with the start of the 1970 model year, illustrates the care taken by Volkswagen of America in the production of its brochures.

The cover of the 1969 model year VW 1600 publication (above left) depicted a green car semi-camouflaged by a green background of grass and trees. The concept behind the brochure's title, "Now can you see yourself in a Volkswagen?" (borrowed from an advert bearing the same strap-line) was both enticing and clever in its declaration that there were cars in the Volkswagen range other than the loathe-it or like-it Beetle.

With the facelift both extending the front of the car by 120mm and changing the style of bumper to the more robust in appearance type originally devised for the Beetle, Volkswagen of America had little option but to provide a new photograph for the 1970 cover (bottom left on page 115). First, they rectified the mistake of green on green, second they selected a picture with more omantic appeal and third, by illuminating the headlamps of the car, they added to its overall visual appearance.

Internal page images such as the example above (top, right) and the particularly atmosphere provoking photograph reproduced on page 115 (bottom, right), also illustrate Volkswagen's duty of car to its products. Note that while tipping the car worked well before the makeover (top, centre), the wider frontal appearance of the revised model might simply have looked obese if such a pose had been adopted.

VW Type 3

The beginning
of an affair

Although the end of production was in sight, the 1973 VW 1600 brochure cover, with its carefully worded title and intriguing image, enticed the showroom browser to discover more, purchase and help fill Volkswagen's sadly depleted coffers.

The Survivor

The Transporter was the only German-built Volkswagen model on the market in both 1970 and 1979, and its US market brochures show a consistent excellence, with ingenuity of design, unmatched word skills, and an evolving variety of styles.

The decade started with the witty brochure, "The car that comes in a box", a 16-page, 216x279mm publication which told the story of the Station Wagon. After all, declared the copywriter, "It's the box that makes it the car it is."

The 16-page black-and-white Truck publication of 1970, "Why your next employee should be a Volkswagen" showcased the very best in American copywriting, while each double-page spread offered a reason why the VW truck should be employed, the language mirroring that used in job descriptions. "They work for less" is reproduced here, while other headlines included: "They work when others can't", (Transporter heading towards a distant building in the midst of a whiteout). "They're resourceful", (Delivery Van squeezing into a small space). "They spend less time away from the job", (Pick-up in for a service). "And they have good references" (Picture of six individuals from different trades with copy in the form of separate testimonials). "Which one should you hire" (picture of each style of VW Truck available). The last heading is self-explanatory – "And after a hard day's work there's a car that lets you get away from it all. The VW Station Wagon."

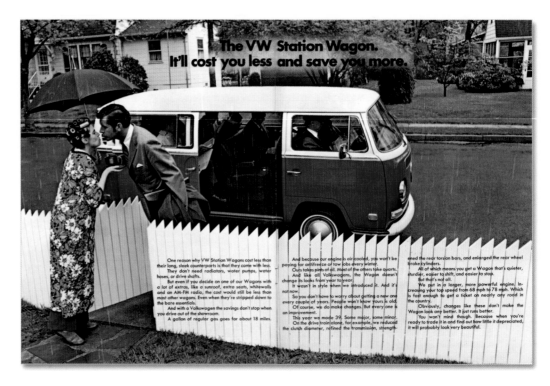

The 1972 model year brochure covering the people carrier was entitled "It's a station wagon more or less".
The cleverness was in the headline accompanying each double spread, including, "It's got more of what you
need and less of what you don't," and, "It holds more people with less crowding".

THE FLOWER BOX

THE BATTER'S BOX

THE TACKLE BOX

THE TOOL BOX

THE ICE BOX

THE MUSIC BOX

THE 1974 VW STATION WAGON. WHO EVER SAID YOU CAN'T TAKE IT WITH YOU?

You've got a problem. Your life is filled with places to go and things to do. But how can you carry all the things you need in a car that's shaped like . . . a car? What you need is a car that's shaped like a box. A box big enough to take you, your family, your friends and your things wherever you want to go.

Easily. Comfortably. Economically.

Try the 1974 VW Station Wagon for size.

With 176 cubic feet of cargo space, you've got room for up to nine people,* a whole lot of gear, or any combination thereof. And nothing was ever easier to load—especially so, with the new fold down rear seat. Slide back the huge side door and start packing. Whether it's a day in the country or a month cross-country you'll have the pleasure of knowing that there's plenty of room for everything and everyone.

And speaking of pleasure, wait 'til you get behind the wheel. First thing you notice is that instead of looking around the car in front of you, you're looking right over it. Now look around you. What do you see? Everything. Eight big windows give you the kind of visibility you've never had before. Three rear-view mirrors allow you to give gas stations a passing glance. That's because your 4-cylinder power plant takes you farther down the road than other wagons. And at today's gasoline prices, that's not just a feature but a blessing.

1974. This is the year you can take it with you. Everything. Everybody. Everywhere.

*Optional seating configuration

THE LUNCH BOX

By 1974 the style had changed somewhat, as an
internal spread from a brochure entitled "The
Gear Box" demonstrates. The pictures quickly
revealed that the Station Wagon was ideal as any
kind of box.....

The more formal – yet still distinctive – approach matured, culminating with the 1977 brochure, "The VW Wagon. It's more than you bargained for". Here, each double page followed the same pattern. On the left, a single photograph; on the right, a series of smaller images that totalled the same amount of space. The text was greater in total wordage, and less idiosyncratic. However, the pages were still appealing and the copy sufficiently different to remain eye-catching.

If you've let the size of your family cause you to make the wrong choice in family transportation, you've missed the Bus. The 1978 Volkswagen Bus.

For all around economy and sheer driving pleasure, you just can't beat the Bus. Nothing else lets you move so much for so little.

The '78 Bus was made for dozens of sensible reasons, as well as for some wonderful fun ones.

The fun starts as soon as you get behind the wheel of your '78 VW Bus. You'll get a good view of the road ahead and the family fun behind.

You'll also get a good feeling knowing that the Bus' peppy fuel-injected engine can give you group rates every time you travel. Because although the Bus is big and quick, it's very economical to operate. In fact, the VW Bus delivers 25 miles per gallon on the highway, and 17 in the city with standard transmission in the 1978 EPA tests. (Of course, your actual mileage may vary depending on where and how you drive, your

Bus' condition and whether you choose optional equipment such as an automatic transmission.)

And what's more, the VW Bus delivers more smiles to the gal-

lon than any other vehicle on the road.

The '78 Bus has hydraulic valve lifters, which give you a quieter engine so your entire gang can sing along with a quiet hum instead of a loud noise.

The '78 VW Bus costs only a little more to buy than the average domestic sedan and less than most big station wagons. For all-around economy, the VW Bus is out in front by miles.

ECONOMICAL FAMILY TRANSPORTATION DOESN'T HAVE TO BE DULL.

A more expansive approach returned with the 1978 publication, a 12-page, 211x276mm brochure, packed with carefully posed imagery epitomised by the cover photograph (above). The Bus is clearly at the heart of the family, with all choosing to help keep it in tip-top condition through regular washing.

IN A WORLD FULL OF SHRINKING WAGONS, IT'S MORE FUN TO TAKE THE BUS.

EVERYONE GETS A SEAT...

For the final year of second generation Transporter production and the 1979 models, Volkswagen of America offered a new style of brochure (cover above) with a landscape, rather than a portrait-style, format. The page count was the same as the previous year, but the marginal increase in size to 307x230mm gave an illusion of generosity. Perhaps the change was determined by the lack of things to say about what was essentially a run-out model. Despite this, the copywriters carefully updated such themes as room for the extended family (top right) and the decidedly vintage story, you can with a Volkswagen bus (right).

THE VERSATILE 1979 BUS...

Presenting
the car of the future.

Having showered customers with lively Beetle brochures packed with customer tributes towards the end of the 1960s, Volkswagen offered a new look for a new decade. After declaring on the cover of the 1970 edition that it was, "Presenting the car of the future," and offering an image of a Beetle in a bubble, the heading on page three tied the car closely to the euphoria surrounding the world's first manned moon landing. "In the future, people will go places they've never been before. VW's are built to take them there."

Other headings were more down to earth, promoting tried-and-tested Beetle values and assets, but with an eye on the future. Typical was the message that ran, "Thanks to an advanced quality control system, VWs have been lasting into the future for years." Back in space, but with an earth landing imminent, was the copy that told of excellent resale values, good fuel economy and the lack of a need for antifreeze, "Which all goes to prove that even in times of skyrocketing costs, you can drive costs down. With our little down-to-earth car."

In the next few years, there'll be
100 million cars on the road.
But there'll always be room for a VW.

Front to rear the Bug measures 13'.
Side to side, 5'.
Which means it can fit into places big dream cars can only dream about.
And weave in and out of traffic with no effort at all.
Especially if you've got our optional automatic stick shift. Because then you can drive around town all day and not change gears.
You also won't have to use the clutch pedal. Because there is none.
Just put it in Drive 1. Sit back and save your strength.
And when you're on the open road and want to cruise over 55 mph, just put it in Drive 2. Sit back and save your gas.
Drive 2 acts like an overdrive. So you can still get about 25 mpg even with the automatic.
(Of course, if you'd rather shift for yourself there's always our standard 4-speed synchromesh transmission.)
And while you're sitting back enjoying the open road, you might want to open your sunroof.
And enjoy the open sky.
You also might want to turn on your AM/FM radio to keep you company.
The sunroof and radio are extras though, so they'll cost a little extra.
But when you consider how much a VW can save you, you may consider treating yourself to a few of life's little extras.

**The Super Beetle.
We've made so many improvements
they're beginning to show.**

**We've designed it for
two types of people.
Men and Women.**

Why have so many women found the VW so easy and so much fun to drive?

One reason is the VW's size: a mere 13 ft. 5 in. long and 5 ft. 2 in. wide.

So it's easier to handle in traffic, easier to make U-turns, and easier to park.

Especially with our optional automatic stick shift.

Then you can drive around town all day without ever changing gears.

There's no clutch pedal. You just put it in Drive 1 and sit back and relax. When you want to cruise over 55 mph, just put it in Drive 2. And that's it.

And the nice thing about our automatic stick shift is that it still lets you get about 25 miles on a gallon of gas.

(Of course, if you'd rather shift for yourself there's always our standard 4-speed synchromesh transmission.)

On the other hand, if you're the man of the house you'll probably like the VW for other reasons.

Like the initial low cost of buying it.

And the air-cooled engine that can never freeze up or boil over. Because it doesn't have a radiator. So it never needs water or antifreeze.

You might also like the fact that it doesn't gulp gas, takes pints of oil instead of quarts, and uses 4 spark plugs instead of 6 or 8.

Then there's VW's high resale value.

And the fast, dependable service you get from any of the over 1,100 VW dealerships in all 50 states.

Of course, the standard equipment the Super Beetle comes with is something everybody will like. Door-to-door carpeting, flow-through ventilation system with a 2-speed blower, bucket seats, telescoping steering column, dual braking system, built-in headrests, day/night rear-view mirror, ignition/steering lock. Even an electric rear-window defogger.

And an automatic control that dims high beams to parking lights whenever the ignition is turned off.

There's also the new big trunk, practically doubled over last year (9.2 vs. 4.9 cu. ft.). Plus, another 4.9 cu. ft. of luggage space behind the rear seat.

Incidentally, if you need more space you can always fold down the back of the rear seat.

Our Super Beetle may not be the most beautiful car in the world. But one thing's for certain.

It's easy to live with.

The US brochure cover for the 1971 model year and the debut of the 1302 range (or Super Beetle as it was known in the USA and elsewhere) was particularly clever. The story was essentially one of a Beetle with more boot space (and new suspension). While the latter was clearly difficult to photograph in any other way than a technical form, to produce a front-section, side profile of the car illustrated perfectly what had happened and showed the re-design from its best angle. A full frontal would have revealed the rather bulbous nature of the boot lid and was therefore reserved for the inside pages. Thus the title of the new brochure sold the story of the latest model to full advantage. "The Super Beetle. We've made so many improvements they're beginning to show."

The internal pages were devoted to delightfully witty headlines and equally highly readable text. Apart from the example above, one of the most intriguing had to be, "We've put on a few more pounds. Now there is more to love".

**The Super Beetle.
The older it gets, the better it gets.**

Such was the success of the 1971 brochure that it was back with an amended title and the odd tweak for a second year. While Wolfsburg appeared to be increasingly ashamed of what was essentially a pre-war design, VW of America paraded the Beetle's lengthy pedigree with pride. "The Super Beetle. The older it gets, the better it gets", proclaimed the cover strap-line (left), while elsewhere the copywriters were confident enough to state that "The Beetle is backed by no less than 24 years of small-car-making experience".

The appearance of the new breed of Super Beetle allowed Volkswagen of America to make greater capital of the lower ranks of Beetle battalions. While neither the 1200 base model, nor the middle-of-the-road VW 1300, were supplied to the USA, a traditional flat-screen Beetle lacking a little bit of brightwork was offered. A four-page black-and-white brochure right) fitted the bill, while its quirky title summed up the car in four simple words.

It goes for less.

The '73 Beetle.
All small cars are not created equal.

Look into the '73 Beetle.
When it comes to quality,
no other small car comes close.

One look at the new Super Beetle for '73 tells you something extraordinary is going on. And in.

It's quality. More of it. To give you more car. To make driving it more of an experience in every way.

Get in, stretch out, and feel the difference for yourself.

You'll discover that VW is thinking bigger than ever before.

The windshield is curved outward and cut higher into the roofline to let in more light and open up the interior. The dashboard is farther away for a feeling of freedom. But the instrument cluster is higher and within easier reach.

Our snazzy new bucket seats are deeper and hold you better on turns. Even the seatbelts are an innovation: they 'give' to give you room to move when you're just riding along. But tighten up automatically when driving conditions tell them to. Most of our competition can't tell you that.

Outside, the taillights have grown to nearly the size of headlights.

Big changes. Small changes: easier to read heating and defrosting controls, better hot and cold air mix. Changes you can't see, like the reinforced bumpers. Plus features we didn't change, features that have already put over 4 million VWs on the American road.

We want to give you quality performance and a quality car.

Always have.

Only this year, we have more to show for it.

For 1973, Volkswagen of America had the task of selling the Super Beetle with a curved windscreen, otherwise know as the 1303. At the centre of the changes were the very un-Beetle-like curved windscreen and an out-of-character, modern plastic dashboard. Here's how the subject was successfully sold: "Get in, stretch out and feel the difference for yourself. You'll discover that VW is thinking bigger than ever before. The windshield is curved outward and cut higher into the roofline to let in more light and open up the interior. The dashboard is further away for a feeling of freedom."

The VW Beetles.
They're built better than ever.

Wolfsburg was heading rapidly towards Passat (Dasher) and Golf (Rabbit) production. The Beetle brochures produced each year after the death knell had been sounded for the car nevertheless illustrated beyond doubt that the American dream was far from over. The 1974 model's cover portrayed the miracle of the car walking on water, something that was actually possible and helped to keep the legend alive.

A Cabriolet-only brochure, again from 1974, included a reminder that the car was "fully equipped with 25 years' worth of sober Volkswagen quality, craftsmanship and reliability". Longevity was being treated as an asset rather than a failure on Wolfsburg's part to move with the times.

The VW Convertible.

One of life's lasting little pleasures.

Some things change.
Some things never change
Volkswagen does both.

The 1975 brochure carried a heading cleverly phrased to illustrate both the experience gained by longevity of production and the process of continual improvement all in one. Inside, headings such as "We've been making the Volkswagen long enough to know better", told the story of '30,000' improvements, while, "An injection for the bug" implied a new lease of life and the accompanying text duly detailed the introduction of fuel injection. The story behind the images and heading reproduced here (right) was one of low depreciation compared to more recent and conceivably less reliable, unproven cars.

Before you put it on the road,
look at it down the road.

Once again, VW
presents the best Beetle
ever built.

The Beetle brochures for 1976 (left) and 1977 models (right) stressed the car's classic nature and the many improvements made to it over the years. There was little else Volkswagen of American could do, as development work back in Germany had virtually ground to a halt. Nevertheless, careful retelling of relatively recent improvements disguised apathy towards the model and allowed a rallying conclusion: "So after 28 years and some 19 million cars, we're happy to report that, this year, we've come up with the almost perfect Beetle."

The Classic Volkswagen.

The Formula Vee Beetle.
It's as much fun to look at as it is to drive.

Actually, the plain, everyday Beetle is fun to drive. Always has been.

Under its mild-mannered appearance lurks a sporty 4-on-the-floor gearshift. Synchromesh transmission. 4-wheel independent torsion bar suspension. Tight, responsive steering.

But it still looks like a plain, everyday Beetle.

So enter the Formula Vee Beetle.

"This is a Beetle?"

A Special Answer to a Problem

The age-old answer to flagging sales was to produce a special, or limited edition, model. A lack of faith in the Beetle at the top ensured that this happened even before sales figures genuinely started to tumble. Predictably, when a special was produced there was a need for a brochure.

Special or limited editions produced by any manufacturer tended to centre on additional trim – life's little luxuries at little or no extra cost. Volkswagen's special Beetles were unquestionably of this ilk. The American market Formula Vee Beetle of 1970/71 illustrated the point perfectly, as it was essentially a straightforward Beetle to which the dealer added a collection of accessories; some items appeared to be part of a great marketing plan, others were optional.

Behold.
A VW Sedan with style.
A Beetle that sings.
With racing stripes along the sides and a Formula Vee decal on the back.
And some things that do more than look good. Take the mag wheel/radial tire combination.
The mags are made of a special aluminum-magnesium-beryllium-titanium alloy. Lightweight. And very strong.
The radials have better sidewall flexing than conventional tires, and put more tread in contact with the road. So they corner better, handle better and minimize aqua-planing on wet roads. They also last longer than conventional tires.

When you're passing, you'll want to let 'em know it. That's why we installed double-toned fanfare horns.
And after you've passed, they'll hear the deep-throated sound of your taper tip dual exhausts. The taper tips reduce exhaust back pressure and help improve gas mileage. And look just great.
Our front hood scoop really scoops. (Some don't.) It pulls in lots of fresh air to keep you and your passengers comfortable.
To keep the body beautiful, we bolted on bumper overriders fore and aft. For more protection on the road or when you're parked.

As flamboyant as we got on the outside...

A British-market special, the GT Beetle, introduced at the end of 1972 to coincide with the sale of the 300,000th Beetle in Britain, was essentially a German-market model in right-hand-drive form with a set of dealer-added extras. The brochure was a clever piece of print for, apart from illustrating all the extra goodies that added no more than £19 to the price, the mostly black-and-white publication carried three blobs of colour to match three new paint shades formulated at Wolfsburg, as applied to the batch of 2500 specials.

Hot property.

The GT Beetle: A very special Beetle at a very special price.

The VW Sports Bug

America's Sports Bug of 1974 was similar in make-up but certainly not identical to Germany's Black and Yellow Racer. Both specials related in their entirety to trim packages. The brochure copywriter couldn't talk of bigger engines, while the designer had to create interest in jazzy decals and what would normally have been extra-cost accessories.

The Jeans Beetle.

Side stripes. | Handy pockets in seat backs. | Sports gear shift. | 3 wave radio. | 4½J Rally wheels. | Tunis yellow body. Cool black exterior trim. | Twin reversing lights. | 1200 power unit. The economical one that lets you cruise at a speed the law doesn't.

In Germany and for many other markets in 1974, the basic 1200 Beetle was supplemented by the young-at-heart, denim-upholstered Jeans Beetle. This came with steel sports wheels, black-painted trim and bumpers rather than chrome or bright alloy, and in Great Britain at least, a paint shade not seen on any other model. Similarly, the curved-screen 1600cc 1303 Beetle attracted a sibling with wider wheels, more upmarket upholstery and trim, plus the odd decal, which became the Big Beetle. For these two specials, very much at the opposite ends of the Beetle spectrum, Volkswagen produced a massive 460x930mm fold-out, poster-style brochure, full of enormous pictures, which no doubt some customers would have found difficult to manhandle.

The Big Beetle.

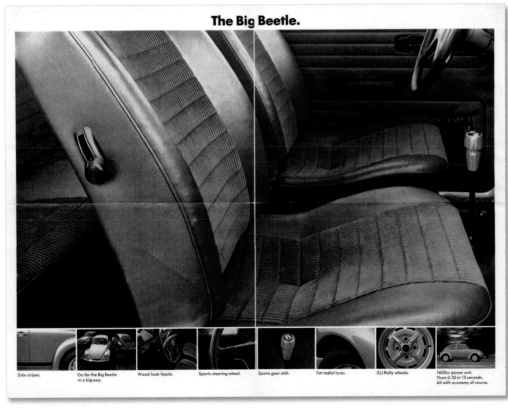

Side stripes. | Go for the Big Beetle in a big way. | Wood-look fascia. | Sports steering wheel. | Sports gear shift. | Fat radial tyres. | 5½J Rally wheels. | 1600cc power unit. Thats 0-50 in 13 seconds. All with economy of course.

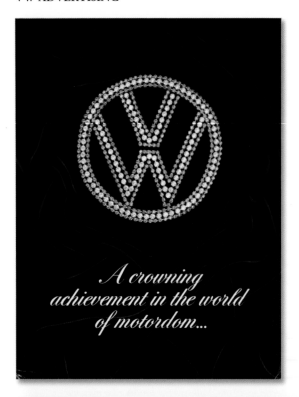

A crowning
achievement in the world
of motordom...

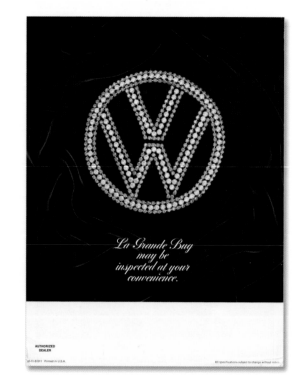

La Grande Bug
may be
inspected at your
convenience.

The US market special edition, "La Grande Bug" was essentially the Big Beetle under a different name, although one or two touches designed to appeal to American tastes were added. A special six page, 215x280mm brochure was produced, although the copywriters had little to say of any significance. The text, reproduced below, both confirms the lack of substance to most special models, while demonstrating the ability of a copywriter to turn very little into a cascade of words:

"For those whose cherished dream has been the prideful ownership of the Ultimate Bug, we offer this superb example of Volkswagen craftsmanship. La Grande Bug. A truly distinguished standard bearer of the VW marque, with amenities not customarily found in a Bug. The rich interior offers special leather grained seating with plush corduroy insets. A leather grained steering wheel. Rosewood appliqué on the dash. An optional tunnel console with matching rosewood appliqué. On the floor, thick, color-cordinated carpeting. Above, a sliding sunroof as standard equipment. Even the body colours cannot be found on any other Bug. Your choice of Ancona Blue Metallic or Lime Green Metallic. With custom silver colored steel wheels as standard equipment..."

Der Weltmeister

Following the demise of the Beetle Saloon in the USA, sales of the Cabriolet increased. Amazingly, Volkswagen responded with various special edition models, one of which extended to the Rabbit (Golf), Dasher (Passat) and even the Transporter (Bus) in both Micro Bus and Campmobile guise. The 28-page brochure was an elaborate affair, as hopefully pages reproduced from it help to illustrate.

The most significant of all special models of the 1970s, "Der Weltmeister" in Germany, the "World Champion" in Britain and for inexplicable reasons, the "Baja Bug" in the USA, lacked its own brochure. Produced to celebrate the Beetle overtaking Model T Ford production numbers in February 1972, owners were offered a package of souvenirs, which, dependent on the country concerned, included a booklet relaying a carefully edited version of the car's history.

Anyone for Golf?

The launch of the VW Passat in 1973 and the VW Scirocco and VW Golf in 1974, might have heralded a change in advertising styles in both Europe and the United States. While the occasional brochure emanating from Wolfsburg appeared to break the mould (as with the first VW Golf publication), the plain cover, pages worked to a template format continued across Europe, just as Volkswagen of America preferred to perpetuate the adventurous trend of lively, well illustrated, but individualistic material.

While it might be suggested that the austere style of promotion adopted in Europe contributed to the decline in popularity of the air-cooled range, such an argument is flawed. The VW Golf and its siblings were an instant success across Europe. Conversely, American dealers struggled with the VW Rabbit and its contemporaries, despite the assumed advantage of dynamic advertising material, brochures that it might well be argued helped to sustain the Beetle and others in their final years.

The first VW Golf brochure.

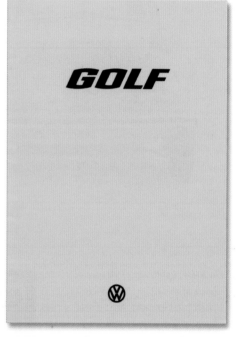

In 1975 there was no change of European policy when it came to plain colour cover brochures.

The 1975 US-market brochure for the VW Rabbit.

The VW Passat became the VW Dasher in the USA. Despite the brochure, sales were hardly shattering.

A 1970s Satellite Story

As the 1970s unfolded, the Transporter increasingly became the mainstay of Heinz Nordhoff's legacy. Sales remained buoyant as those of the Beetle declined and other models ceased production.

Just as Volkswagen of America produced a wealth of material in their own distinctive style to promote the Transporter and other models, so did Volkswagen's many satellite operations. None seemed eager to adopt Wolfsburg's plain cover, template driven approach.

Volkswagen of Australia's 1973 Transporter brochure (right) was a relatively simple 12-page black and white affair. Measuring 210x266mm, it relied on at least a percentage of photography common to European brochures, while the carefully written, but on occasion slightly humdrum, text was more in keeping with US length, merely lacking its renowned wit. The eye-catching cover headline, "More power to the workers" referred to the optional 1700cc engine, which must have come as something of a disappointment to the brochure browsers.

In 1975, Volkswagen of Brazil was still manufacturing its own version of the first generation Transporter, a vehicle of the style that had ceased production in Germany at the end of July 1967. The brochure to promote the Kombi, as all models were referred to, carried a minimum of text across its six 209mm x 290mm pages, while only two featured imagery of the vehicles. Instead, the cover and three consecutive fold out pages were devoted to the single message of the Kombi being a "work-leisure car", with the pictorial evidence very much in favour of lifestyle and leisure rather than any trace of work.

Although the South African satellite's production varied in minor details from German output, generally its reputation was one of staid conformity. While brochure output wasn't identical to that of 1970s Wolfsburg, neither did it meander in the direction of American output. Instead, a typical South African publication such as the 1978 Transporter one illus-

trated here bore more than a passing resemblance to late 1960s and early 1970s brochures, such as those featured on pages 134 and 135. The 1978 brochure not only conformed to such a look but was also of a typical 210mm x 297mm size. A total of 12 pages was likewise an accepted standard number. The text appeared at first glance to be lengthy until it was appreciated that each spread was devoted to two columns in English and a further couple in Dutch. Having said that, the style of copywriting was hardly dynamic and lacked the polished appeal mastered by Doyle Dane Bernbach in the United States.

"More power to the workers" in this 1973 Australian brochure referred to the optional 1700c engine.

VW Light Commercials, a brochure printed in Brazil in English to promote the 1975 range of Kombis, placed great emphasis on life surrounding the vehicles.

Kombi 1600 and 1600L – today's best 10-seater value

Meet the best-selling 10-seaters in South Africa: Volkswagen's Kombi and Microbus range. And for 1978 they're better than ever.

For a start there's the Kombi 1600 – by far the lowest priced 10-seater in the country. Handsome and rugged, the Kombi 1600 features all the specific advantages that make a Volkswagen a Volkswagen. Like a guarantee that covers you for a full 12 months – irrespective of kilometres travelled. Independent suspension on all four wheels for a ride like a car's. All the luxury touches you'd expect of a car, including a heater. Enter through the robust, wide swing-open side doors and you have twice the seating capacity of an average car. And twice the luggage space: 991 dm³, accessible through a swing-up door at the rear. All in a vehicle that, amazingly, is less than half a metre longer than

a little VW Beetle. So parking in small spaces is child's play.

Then for a little more money you can get our Kombi 1600L. For 1978 it boasts a host of new improvements. Like new vinyl trim panels, bonded seat covers, added sound insulation, reverse lights, an anti-dazzle rear-view mirror and a padded steering wheel. And of course you get a wide sliding side door and a walk-through aisle between the front seats.

Yet with these new refinements the Kombi 1600L remains a Volkswagen. And all that that has come to mean. Behind both our Kombi's is Volkswagen's latest 1600 cm³ engine. Which means ample power plus the kind of economy and low-revving reliability that only a Volkswagen can give you.

Kombi 1600 en 1600L – 10-sitplek-busse met die hoogste waarde vandag

Volkswagen se reeks Kombi's en Mikrobusse is al klaar die 10-sitplek- voertuie met die beste afset in Suid-Afrika vandag. En nou is die van 1978 nog beter.

Kom ons begin met die Kombi 1600 – verreweg die billikste 10-sitplekwa tans in die land. By sy mooiheid en gehardheid besit hy al die spesifieke voordele wat 'n Volkswagen 'n Volkswagen maak. Soos 'n waarborg vir 'n volle 12 maande, al ry u ook hoe ver. Onafhanklike vering aan al vier wiele wat hom nes 'n motor laat ry. Al die weeldergehede wat u in 'n motor sou verwag – verwarmer inbegrepe. Maak die sterk, wye oopswaai-sydeure oop en voor u is daar dubbel die sitruimte van 'n gemiddelde motor. Ook het hy dubbel die bagasieruimte: 991 dm³, met toegang deur 'n opswaaideur agter. Dit alles in 'n voertuig wat, verbasend genoeg, skaars 'n halwe meter

langer as die klein VW-Kewertjie is. Parkering in beperkte ruimtetjies is dus kinderspeletjies.

Dan, vir 'n bietjie meer geld, kan u ons Kombi 1600L kry. Die 1978-model het vele nuwe verbeterings. Soos nuwe vinielpanele, gebinde sitplekoortreksels, ekstra klankisolering, truligte, 'n blikkinvry truspieël en 'n gestoffeerde stuurwiel. En natuurlik kry u ook 'n wye skuif-sydeur en 'n deurgang tussen die voorste sitplekke.

By al hierdie nuwe verfyndhede, egter, bly die Kombi 1600L nog steeds Volkswagen. Met alles wat die naam inhou.

Agter albei ons Kombi's sit Volkswagen se jongste laasnelheidsenjin van 1600 cm³. Dit beteken oorgenoeg krag plus die soort besparing en betroubaarheid wat slegs Volkswagen u kan gee.

The 1978 South African Transporter brochure included an appealing if deliberately slightly out of focus cover, while the double spread reproduced here concentrated on a Transprter imported from Brazil, although no references to its origins were made in the text. (No South African or German second generation Transporter featured first generation side-loading doors.).

... And Finally

Although the Beetle didn't die when the last German-built car left the Emden factory in January 1978, the story of its promotion through brochures was entering the final chapter. Until 1985, Beetles were imported from Mexico to Germany and other selected European countries. The brochures remained virtually identical to those of earlier swansong years, but there was a notable exception, which came in the form of material to celebrate a series of limited edition models. In the tradition of specials from earlier years, all offered little more than special paint colours, additional trim or decals, in some instances sports wheels and luxurious upholstery.

The 1984 Sunny Beetle, "Aussen sonnig. Innen wonnig" (Sunny outside. Blissful inside) again sported a special shade of exterior paint and rather bright upholstery inside.

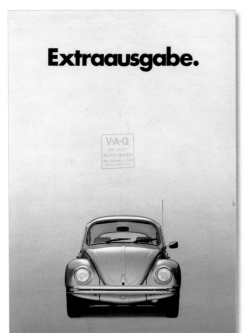

The four-page 1985 brochure promoting "Der letze Käfer" largely followed the format of its predecessors. However, the discreetly decaled car, with its special Zinngraue Metallic paint, was also promoted as the 50-year Beetle and the Jubilee model.

Dated September 1983, this four-page brochure was designed to promote the Winter Beetle, a special edition finished in Ice Blue Metallic paint with matching upholstery.

1984 specials included the Velvet Red model, "Die neueste Sonderausgabe. Der samtrote Sonderkäfer" (The latest Special Edition. The Velvet red special Beetle). The brochure, dated June 1984 highlighted the paint colour and matching velour upholstery and "petal" decals on the car's lower side panels.

Der letzte Käfer.

Kein Auto auf der Welt ist so bekannt wie der Käfer. Er kennt keine Klassenunterschiede, er ist kein Statussymbol. Seit 50 Jahren sieht der Käfer unverkennbar wie ein Käfer aus. Ein halbes Jahrhundert wurde er gebaut, fast 21 millionenmal ver- kauft. Einsame Weltrekorde in der Geschichte des Automobils. Jetzt gibt's ein Happy-End. Der Käfer verabschiedet sich von seinem Millionen-Publikum. Mit den letzten 2.400 Exemplaren seiner Art. Exklu- siv und sportlich ausgestattet, wie Sie hier selbst nachlesen können. Zwar verschwindet der Käfer aus unseren Volkswagen-Prospekten und aus dem Schauraum der V. A. G Part- ner. Aber auf unseren Straßen wird er weiter fahren. Noch ein ganzes Weilchen.